As I Remember It

BOOKS BY JAMES BRANCH CABELL

Biography of the Life of Manuel
Beyond Life · Figures of Earth · The Silver Stallion · The Witch-Woman · Domnei · Chivalry · Jurgen · The Line of Love · The High Place · Gallantry · Something About Eve · The Certain Hour · The Cords of Vanity · From the Hidden Way · The Jewel Merchants · The Rivet in Grandfather's Neck · The Eagle's Shadow · The Cream of the Jest · The Lineage of Lichfield · Straws and Prayer-Books · Townsend of Lichfield, Preface to the Past, Between Dawn and Sunrise (*with* John Macy)

The Nightmare Has Triplets
Smirt · Smith · Smire

Heirs and Assigns
Hamlet Had an Uncle · The King Was in His Counting House · The First Gentleman of America

It Happened in Florida
The St. Johns (*with* A. J. Hanna) · There Were Two Pirates · The Devil's Own Dear Son

Their Lives and Letters
These Restless Heads · Special Delivery · Ladies and Gentlemen

Virginians Are Various
Let Me Lie · Quiet, Please · As I Remember It

Upon Genealogy
Branchiana · Branch of Abingdon · The Majors and Their Marriages

X, Y & Z
The Judging of Jurgen · Joseph Hergesheimer · Taboo · The Music from Behind the Moon · Ballades from the Hidden Way · The White Robe · The Way of Ecben · Sonnets from Antan · Some of Us · The Nightmare Has Triplets (*pamphlet*) · Of Ellen Glasgow, An Inscribed Portrait (*with* Ellen Glasgow)

As I Remember It

Some Epilogues in Recollection

by

James Branch Cabell

"I am a part of all that I have met."

THE McBRIDE COMPANY
New York

Copyright 1955 by
JAMES BRANCH CABELL

Library of Congress Catalog Card Number: 55-11765

Printed in the United States of America

Published simultaneously in Canada by
BURNS & MACEACHERN
Toronto

Contents

A FOREWORD:
AS TO WHAT COMES LATER

> "Just as writers ought to do
> On attempting to make clear
> How they came to write, so here
> Nothing shall be hid from you."

My dear John Farrar:

For a great while now it has been my desire to inscribe a book to you as the formal token of my large indebtedness and of our long friendship. Herewith I fulfil that desire.

I would not, for a variety of reasons, have chosen the present volume except for the overwhelming reason that I know this in all likelihood to be the last book I shall ever complete. So it is now or never, remarks common sense a bit grimly.

You have hereinafter a dissertation which concerns itself throughout its little length with matters, and with people also, that I like to remember. It, in most instances, records yet furthermore how they have collaborated with or have entered into my writings.

That my catalogue is fragmentary and all but haphazard is best shown by the fact that you, my dear Farrar, do not figure in it as my editorial arbiter and beneficent censor throughout eleven years' space. There, by rights, should be a full chapter about you.

"And there should be another one about Richard Butler Glaenzer," my conscience here interrupts me. "And besides that, you have left out Marjorie Rawlings and Howard Pyle and Burton Rascoe. You have not spoken of Henry Mills Alden or of Robert M. McBride. Nor is there as much as a word about Earl Emmons—"

"I know," I reply meekly; "but one cannot have everything."

And thereupon—because not even a raging abstraction may contend against triteness—thereupon my conscience turns tail and skuttles back sulkily to wherever it sleeps by ordinary.

This book, then, deals with but a few of my collaborators in the making of numerous books, all of whom I remember with amusement and pleasure and in most instances with affection. It follows no plan more complex in any place. It had started life as two separate volumes when I noted that one of them had been builded in an unconscious but an absolute accord with the specifications outlined for the other one of them—videlicet, for me to write about affairs and persons that I like to remember—and I, in consequence, blended the two.

I have found the task heart-warming, thus to recall in my life's evening some of my life's so very many, very simple amenities. Yet I fear the resultant book must seem, in the opinion of its younger readers, to be a superfluous and, indeed, a somewhat naively recorded medley of recollections which are of no importance nowadays, not to anybody anywhere, except only to him who assembled them—and a medley into which, as a yet further detriment, its assembler has been so crude as to introduce an element of candor.

For that to admit this quality into a volume of reminiscences, of whatsoever weight, is not customary, I must grant. To be candid in print concerning one's intimates, or concerning one's acquaintances, ranks as sentimentality, or as bad taste, or as backbiting, and more often than seldom, as the three commingled; whereas to be candid about one's own doings, or emotions, or opinions, is egotism.

Now, obviously, a writer ought to avoid any such deplorable vices. And so, when he becomes reminiscent as to the more vital features of his living, it is preferable he should recollect, first of all, that the truth about his memories needs for the most part to be omitted; and as goes the remainder, to be edited into, and continuously recolored with, the civilities of fiction.

I concede, however, that I have not always pursued this proper course hereinafter. It follows in logic that—here and there at least—I must have been betrayed into egotism and backbiting and bad taste, as well as into sentimentality, as the price of candor. I am suitably sorry.

And with that still-candid admission, my dear Farrar, do you permit me to subscribe myself—as always—

Yours faithfully,
James Branch Cabell

August 24, 1955

Book One:

Another Book About Her

"They have all forgotten. They all insist today that you were an angel, and they have come almost to believe that you habitually flew about the world in a nightgown, with an Easter lily in your hand. . . . But I remember, dear."

1

Which Tells You How It All Started

Our first formal meeting I do not remember. But when in 1912, as was then my habit every year, I returned to the Rockbridge Alum Springs in the early summer—toward the end of June, I imagine—I had been introduced to a Mrs. Somebody-or-Other Shepherd, from Somewhere, it might have been a day or perhaps two days before the afternoon I came out upon the low platform in front of the Central Hotel a fair while before supper time. Very few people were about as yet. The broad lawn before the hotel was deserted.

She was sitting alone upon the trellised porch of the fifth cottage from the hotel, to the right hand side of me. I remember how, at that not inconsiderable distance, I noted the free and proud poise of her head when you saw it thus in profile. I remember how I walked across the lawn, through the prolonged shadows of sunset, in order to talk with her.

I do not know what moved me to do this. I can re-

3

call only that it seemed natural, and in some vague sense it seemed inevitable, for me to be going to this woman, about whom I knew nothing at all except that she was a Mrs. Somebody-or-Other Shepherd from Somewhere.

I was surprised when I found out that, like me, she lived in Richmond, or at least upon the northern out-skirts of Richmond, in a suburb called Dumbarton, which I had heard of but had never seen. And her husband, it developed, was dead. Or perhaps I already knew of her widowhood. I am not positive.

What trifles we may have talked about until it was time to go in to supper at the hotel I do not recollect. But I know nowadays that, during this talk upon her cottage porch facing the sunset, I became fond of her. I began to regard her with affection.

I am not saying I fell in love with Mrs. Emmett A. Shepherd thus instantly. In fact, as I have admitted over and over again, I am not certain, upon looking back on my youth, that I ever "fell in love" with any-body after the romanticists' high fashion which I so often have both read and written about with enjoy-ment. But to a heart-warming degree did I approve of the prettiness of this slender and brown-haired and dark-eyed woman. I viewed favorably the way in which, almost always, just before she began to speak she would smile suddenly and brightly.

Such, so I found out later, was her habit in speaking with virtually everyone; and it sprang from the fact that she liked her fellow creatures. She was friendly with every person instinctively until that person had injured her, or had offended her in one or another manner, or had done something of which she felt with an urgency called on to disapprove. Which does not mean that the range of her disapproval was niggardly. She was a wholly competent disapprover. And when, as Mrs. Shepherd phrased it, she was disappointed in a person, then she was through with that person. Dame Lisa said the same thing, five years afterward, in a book called *Jurgen*.

And I delighted in Mrs. Shepherd's slurring, soft, but so quietly self-assured, quaint manner of speaking. It seemed quaint, and indeed uniquely odd, at this time, I mean. Later, I found out that she spoke as all her people had always spoken in Charles City County since 1619 or thereabouts, for they had settled in Charles City before this county, or in fact any other county in Virginia, was christened; and to the collo-quialisms of Charles City, as I learned also later on, she adhered invincibly.

Well, but that quiet, sunset-lighted, uneventful-seeming afternoon was the beginning of my interest in her. Yet there was no excitement, and no deepness, in my feeling for this not unattractive young woman, at first. At first, my emotion was but a pleased response, I suppose, to her instinctive and impersonal friendli-ness toward the entire human race.

As to what was her first sentiment toward me I was never told by the one person who knew anything about it. I think, though, it was curiosity. She had been fore-

warned by the legends of my native city, as she admitted later, that in addition to being the writer of some
highfaluting books nobody ever thought of wasting any
time on (when I might have kept a perfectly good
newspaper job except for my complete worthlessness),
I was likewise a murderer spared only so as to prevent
a family scandal, as well as being a sexual pervert, a
seducer of womanhood at large, a sponger upon my
well-to-do relatives, an habitual drunkard, and a practitioner of I, at this distance in time, forget just what
other misdemeanors. Richmond was never over gentle
with my repute.

So it seemed sort of curious, right in the beginning,
to be talking with me on her own front porch, even
though of course she had not ever believed quite all
of it. Such is the extent of my information.

At any rate, we were very often together during the
rest of that tranquil summer at the Rockbridge Alum
Springs. We found we liked being together. We talked
about nothing in particular, and we talked with an
exceeding contentment, did Mrs. Emmett A. Shepherd
and I, during that faraway summer when Mr. Taft was
President.

Well, and during the preceding twelve summers I
had been enamoured of a number of young women at
the Rockbridge Alum (where virtually every patron,
excepting only the age-stricken, indulged in, at least,
one love-affair every "season"), so that the place was,
of necessity, memory-haunted. Under this or the other

tree, or upon yonder venerable and secluded bench, or in some special part of the rambling lawns, or in any one of the four spring houses, by moonlight usually, there had been amorous dealings which I remembered with clearness; and I recalled also in which of the Central Hotel's or of the Brook's or of the cottages' bed-rooms, and during which particular summer, toward impassioned midnights, I had figured as an unlegalized guest. But the odd part of it to me was that, now, all these ecstatic and sometimes technically iniquitous but in each case so very vividly recollected antics appeared so unimportant. I felt, now, that Mrs. Emmett A. Shepherd alone mattered.

Yet I did not make any physical advances to Mrs. Emmett A. Shepherd, nor did I declare verbally how much I adored Mrs. Emmett A. Shepherd. For I was not, I protest, I was not at this time that which we call "in love" with her. My feeling toward Mrs. Emmett A. Shepherd was, rather, that I had become more fond of this brown-haired woman than ever in my life I had been of any other person. To be with her begot in me—just somehow—a dispassionate, and an unreasoned, but a wholly dear contentment.

2

Ends by Discrediting Superstition

IT WAS at this time I first wrote about her, in the short story called "A Brown Woman." I have been re-reading this story lately, and not in its final version but in its unrevised original magazine form, just as I put it together in 1912.

The tale tells, I find, how a professional writer (whom artfully I disguised as a poet obsessed by his desire to write perfectly about beautiful happenings) encountered a brown-haired young woman—brown hair with gold in it—whose main concerns were not with literature; who had never read his books, or for that matter, any other books; and it tells how his love for her began.

"I wish," one finds this writer saying, "I wish I could make you understand how your coming has changed everything."

And it is that, it is that precisely, which today, at

8

this instant, I am trying to make comprehensible, but above all, to myself, now the doings of 1912 appear as remote as the glories of Charlemagne or of Achilles.

Afterward the tale goes on to say: "It seemed to him he could never tire of noting her excellences. Perhaps it was that splendid light poise of her head he chiefly loved; he thought so just now at least. Or was it the wonder of her walk, which made all other women he had ever known appear to mince and hobble, like rusty toys? Something there was assuredly about this slim brown girl which recalled an untamed and harmless woodland creature; and it was that, he knew, which most poignantly moved him, even though he could not name it. Perhaps it was her bright, kind eyes, which seemed to mirror the tranquillity of forests. . . ."

That is how Mrs. Emmett A. Shepherd appeared to me in those days. That was done upon the spot, from life. That is, so do I still believe, a true enough portrait, howsoever superficial and fragmentary (and in need of some verbal retouching, so I decided later) of this young Mrs. Shepherd as she was at the time of our meeting, even though for the tale's sake I was compelled to lessen her age handsomely, presenting her as a girl of eighteen. And it records at any rate just how I thought about her.

Then toward the end of my story I find the writer whom it concerns to be saying:—

"So she is dead. It is very strange. So many rare felicities of curve and color, so much of purity and kindliness and valor and mirth, extinguished as one snuffs a candle! Well! I am sorry she is dead, for she had a talent for living and got such joy out of it. . . . Hers was a lovely happy life, but it was sterile. Already nothing remains of her but dead flesh which must be huddled out of sight.

"I shall not perish thus entirely, I believe. Men will remember me. . . .

"Truly, a mighty foundation for pride! when the utmost I can hope for is but to be read in one island, and to be thrown aside at the end of one age. Indeed, I am not even sure of that much. I print, and print, and print. And when I collect my verses into books, I am altogether uncertain whether to look upon myself as a man building a monument, or burying the dead. It sometimes seems to me that each publication is but a solemn funeral of many wasted years. For I have given all to the verse-making. Granted that the sacrifice avails to rescue my name from oblivion, what will it profit me when I am dead and care no more for men's opinions than she cares now for what I say of her?"

Whereafter, so the story records, this writer dipped pensively his pen into his inkwell. And he set about writing as to the death of that kindly and valorous, brown-haired woman whom he had loved, as being (because of its unusual circumstances) a quaint theme such as was not unworthy to be commemorated in his Complete Works.

Very certainly in this tale, as I first typed it out in the autumn of 1912, I can find nowadays a vast deal more of irony than ever anybody meant, consciously, to put into it.

I boggle, though, over the phrase, "Her life was sterile." And with candor must I admit that an author's vainglory, it is possible, begets this hesitance, or at any rate, strengthens it, inasmuch as I know that from the midsummer of 1912 onward, this brown-haired, soft-voiced but emphatic woman entered into virtually everything I wrote; she contributed to never so many of the feminine characters in my never so many books; and she provided me with glad reams of phrases very far beyond my inventiveness. Then by-and-by she made more facile the writing of every line that I got down on paper throughout some thirty-five years, those so remote seeming years during which her protectiveness enabled me to revise all the short stories and the novels I had published before I knew her.

It follows that so long as any of these writings may happen to endure, she must be ranked as their co-author. And I find it pleasing to reflect that anybody could have been the co-author of some forty-odd books without ever having been put to the trouble, so do I still suspect, of needing to read any one of them.

I cannot figure how long we had known each other before, upon the evening of the twelfth of August in 1912—because about that date I am certain—we drove over to attend a german at the Alleghany Hotel in

Goshen; and after our return, toward midnight, from these staid gaieties, we sat upon her cottage porch for a while, just where I had first seen her, still talking about nothing in particular, or at least about nothing which I now remember.

But I do remember it was then that without any conscious premeditation I put my arm about her in the midsummer-smelling darkness, and I kissed her. There was in this action nothing erotic. It was hardly amorous. I kissed her just because I was very, very fond of her.

She did not pretend to be surprised or shocked, as in such circumstances was the role of a gentlewoman in those days. She did not mention that she had thought I had more respect for her. Instead, we both accepted that first kiss as being far less anything which we were doing than as being something which was happening to the two of us, in a measureless darkness, unviolently, unavoidably.

"No good, though, can come of any such behavior, ma'am," I then observed with severity; "for it is now the thirteenth."

That is the first thing which I can definitely remember saying to Mrs. Emmett A. Shepherd. And in saying it I, for this once at any rate, was mistaken. All that which for a long while afterward was best in my living began upon that special thirteenth of August.

3

Relates What Happened Before
1912

WHEN she was born in Charles City County, some thirty-odd years before we met each other, it had happened a little bit ahead of time, upon account of her mother's having tried to chase a cow out of the front yard. And her father was one of the Bradleys of Auburn.

He was the very best farmer that anybody ever knew. He could tell from looking at a sunset just what the weather was going to be for the next day, or for the next several days; and in farming, it appears, any such advance information is of large value.

But Father had died when he was only forty-two. He was survived by a widow and four children and regrettably few other visible belongings. Mr. William Joseph Bradley of Auburn, in between his so accurate evaluations of sunsets, I learned to infer, was not always an exact or over-insistent prohibitionist. I was never told as much. Charles City has a way of conveying harsh facts without stating them bluntly.

That was why Mother came up to Richmond and started to take in boarders, down on East Broad Street. It was a boarding house everybody remembered who ever stopped at it. It had been conducted, however, upon a scale so lavish—thus yet again did I infer—and so thoroughly in accord with the liberal plantational customs of Charles City, and it had been so very backward about troubling its patrons to pay their board until they found this action to be wholly convenient, because in Charles City County a lady was not supposed to come after people about money, that this boarding house did not thrive financially.

But everybody like staying there; and everybody loved Mother Bradley, as almost every one of her boarders called Mother. Mother was one of the Waddills of Roxbury.

So the older Miss Bradley—or Miss Rebecca Priscilla Bradley, to be precise—decided she ought to go to work. And after that, she did the typewriting for Mr. Hill Montague, in his offices at Tenth and Main Street, just across from McAdams & Berry.

She remembered my uncle by marriage, Mr. McAdams, very well, because he was one of the most handsome men that anybody ever saw anywhere; and he nearly always wore a light gray suit of clothes, with a red flower on the lapel of it. Mrs. McAdams used to drive down for him almost every afternoon, in a little surrey, with a bright yellow horse to it, so as to keep

Mr. McAdams from stopping at the Commonwealth Club before he went home for his supper. Or at any rate, that was what everybody said was why.

All this was in the middle 1890's, not long before Miss Rebecca Priscilla Bradley, only her friends called her Miss Percie Bradley, met the Mr. Emmett A. Shepherd whom in due course, in 1896, she married. He was just the finest man in the world, and always so considerate, too. He was really wonderful.

So they had two children upon West Avenue; and Mr. Shepherd began to do better and still better in the lumber business. He was splendid at it, for he knew all about timber, even if you did have to keep right behind him all the time, because he was so easily discouraged and so apt to think everybody was down on him.

Well, then, but after that (with the lumber business thus prospering), after that, they had bought from old Major Courtney a place out in the country, at Dumbarton, with enough land to do a little farming on, and mostly upon account of poor Isabelle. There they had three more children before Mr. Shepherd got the most awful sort of eye trouble and died in the January of 1910.

His Masonic lodge and all the people who knew him wrote absolutely wonderful letters about it. There was a big portfolio full of them, back at home, in Dumbarton.

4

Appears Mostly About Nomenclature

So MUCH, then, did a brown-haired and slender and quietly self-certain and, to my finding, a remarkably pretty Mrs. Shepherd tell me in the summer of 1912. And she had decided not to marry me, because she was older than I was, a good four and a half years, and especially on account of the children. She thought it would not be fair to them. She felt she owed it to them to give up the rest of her life to taking care of her children, quite apart from poor Isabelle's being an invalid.

Well, but as I pointed out later, and as I repeated time and again during the years which followed, I had not said anything whatever about our getting married. I had not proposed to her. I explained that I never did propose to her. It was merely, so did I protest, that when an obtuse Mrs. Emmett A. Shepherd, from the backwoods of Charles City County somewhere, announced it would be better for her not to marry me—who was no mere Bradley of Auburn but a

16

Cabell of Cayford, I reminded her, with chill conde-
scension—then my hurt pride, and my common-sense
likewise, had led me to dispute any such nonsense.

I have contended also that when I married an extremely strong-willed widow with five children, for four
of whom a continual argufying (as Charles City termed
it) was their pet diversion, I ought to have been awarded
the Carnegie medal for bravery. It still puzzles me that
my marriage did not result as do the marriages of so
many professional writers, or at least their first two or
three marriages, because my wife and I did not ever
have anything in common except only a certain fondness for each other.

We kept that always; and in particular did we keep
the certainness of it. I like to remember that.

Now of these five children, the oldest one—born
upon West Avenue, and called Isabelle, which was
after Mr. Shepherd's mother of course, and she really
was just the brightest baby that you ever saw anywhere
—had been stricken, when barely three years old, with
infantile paralysis. After which she developed into girlhood as a witless and inarticulate fragment of wreck-
age, unable to move the lower half of her body. And,
in consequence, Isabelle had to be fed and tended by
her Negro nurse, large, blatant, large-voiced Martha
Cousins, who intended to be made simply a door mat
of by no white folks anywhere so long as she was able
to walk straight out of this house.

Never at any time after my wife's second marriage,

it may be added, did Martha Cousins consent to speak
of or to address my wife except as Mrs. Shepherd. And
never during my earthly existence have I been hated so
actively, or so wholly without concealment, as by
Martha Cousins during the years that followed my
marriage.

But otherwise, I believe, I fitted smoothly enough
into the extensive family circle which I had acquired
overnight; and my four other stepchildren—from a perplexed unease as to the so very many dreadful things
which Martha Cousins predicted, volubly and without
any cessation, I was going to do to them right off when
once that crazy mother of theirs had simply killed herself by marrying me—the children, I repeat, passed
from a reserved suspicion into tolerance, and thence,
I think, into a fair amount of affection. That was my
wife's doing, I know, for she managed everyone of us
—even Martha Cousins, almost—forthrightly, with tact,
blandly, unswervingly.

For one example, ever since we first talked together
in the summer sunset, my wife had spoken freely and
with a serene fondness as to Mr. Shepherd and her
reminiscences of him; and that led to my misconduct
eventually, during the following July, or thereabouts,
after our marriage in November. I do not at all remember what prefaced my rudeness. I recall only that of a
sudden I told her, with a candor which irritation fla-
vored spleenishly, that I did not want ever to hear any
more about the man.

And my prompter was jealousy, I concede; but a special sort of jealousy. For I did not mind her having loved him. I do not think I was ever jealous of his role in her past. I most certainly did not resent the so tangible mementoes of this role, in the form of five children, for I had come to regard these children with a fondness which was not remote from paternal. Then, too, I admitted to myself in private—fair-mindedly enough, I thought, and with what I tried to think was remorse—that during the years of her married life with Mr. Shepherd, I had cherished a number of injudicious young women, about whom I had omitted to tell my wife. But for the usual precautions of a bachelor in any such tender affairs, I also during this period might have started a family or two, I granted.

No; rather was I jealous of my wife's unhidden admiration of Mr. Shepherd as an ornament to the lumber trade, and to his Masonic lodge, and to business circles —he was even in the Virginia State Chamber of Commerce—and to the vestry of Emmanuel Church, and to the community of Dumbarton and the city of Richmond at large. Rather did I deplore her tacit assumption that, when compared with these high glories, the writing of books was a perhaps harmless but, after all, a somewhat childish performance. For while an author may suspect this much at bottom, and find logic to back him, yet he does not enjoy having other persons regard this forlorn suspicion as a granted truism.

So I said, with an absurd flare of petulance, that she talked about her Mr. Emmett A. Shepherd—to whom

I may even have applied an adjective—simply all the time (which by a large deal was diverse from being true, as I conceded in private at the same instant I was saying it), and that, for one, I did not want ever to hear any more about the man.

She looked at me pensively, I can remember—in surprise at first, and then with a maternal, with an almost smiling, forgiveness. But she said only, with quietude, that Mr. Shepherd had always been a wonderful husband to her, and that she did not see what on earth there was to fuss about and to swell up like a toad frog. So then I kissed her. And we, well, we eventually, we let it go at that.

Nevertheless, I observed, from that time on she referred to Mr. Shepherd, within my hearing, very far less frequently. She did not ever again extol to me his multitudinary virtues. And I knew, half-frettedly, that in this matter also, my wife was indulging my just plain out-and-out childishness, as Charles City County would have phrased it. I reflected that, at bottom, the memory of him remained to my wife supremely dear, do what I might.

I have need to speak of her thus formally as "my wife," because while her intimates had abbreviated Priscilla into Percie, and they all addressed her in this way, I did not ever learn to do so. I do not know why. Nor during our first acquaintance, to the best of my recollection, did I ever call her Mrs. Shepherd. I instead said "you."

So nowadays, in the event of my speaking of her to persons with whom she was upon familiar terms, I referred to her as Percie just as they did. Yet whenever I spoke to my wife, either in private or publicly, I continued to say "you," or now and then perhaps "my dear," or it might be "darling," or in extreme cases—so I would boast at any rate—"you hellion."

But she of course, after we were married, then she began to call me Mr. Cabell, because in Charles City that was the correct way for a wife to speak to her husband. When I objected, she replied in a vein of calm surprise that she had always called Mr. Shepherd Mr. Shepherd. But that, I protested, had nothing to do with it; and so, after some unembittered argument, my wife consented to resume calling me by my first name —although with a frank sense of awkwardness and of behaving somewhat immodestly—just as she had done before we were married.

She became accustomed to this breach of Charles City's decorum, by-and-by, gradually. She learned how to say James without actually blushing. And it was only when my obtuseness had appeared to her beyond human endurance that she would begin instead with a "But, my darling," spoken in a tone of voice for which no unabridged dictionary can provide a describing. It made, though, of the word "darling" an unmistakable but a friendly enough synonym for "idiot." She could not resist being friendly with everybody, even an irrational husband.

And a husband so abysmally irrational, and as

Charles City phrased it, so pernickety, that he had tried to lay down the law for people who did not intend to be bossed by any man alive about their own names.

This means that, although by her friends and her relatives my wife had always been called Percie, yet up to the time of our marriage she had chosen to sign her legal name as Rebecca P. Shepherd. Well, and it developed that the misguided woman was now planning, without any perceptible qualms, to become a Rebecca P. Cabell. She told me so herself.

Forthwith I declined, with indignation, and upon all imaginable terms, to consort with an atrocity thus cacophonous. And for once at least, this being our honeymoon period, I was allowed to have my own way without any particular disputation.

I, in brief, now rechristened Mr. Shepherd's young widow completely; and because of my so foolish, just simple, plain pig-headedness about nothing whatever (it was mentioned in passing), she agreed to be known henceforward as Priscilla Bradley Cabell.

That was the first essential change which I made at our home out in the country at Dumbarton.

5

Here Work Begins on My Masterpiece

A<small>ND</small> I introduced into our home at Dumbarton some yet other innovations, now that I had started to trace out, with an ever-growing interest and no little pride, this Priscilla Bradley Cabell's background and her forefathers in Charles City County. I found it gratifying to discover with how many and how very upper classes I had intermarried.

Our anonymous house and its modest farm lands meanwhile—through what I still consider to have been a stroke of genius—had been christened Dumbarton Grange. And with that unassuming, yet not unself-confident, name we began to conform in our home's atmosphere.

The portraits and the silhouettes and the daguerreotypes of my wife's family, along with their Early Victorian furniture and whatnots and demure, bright figurines and the Doulton pottery and the Wedgwood

pottery, and in brief the Bradleys' put-by "parlor orna-
ments" in general, were released from long years of seclusion in the attic. Some of them henceforward kept
quaint our dining room and our drawing room. But the
majority were arranged—not ineffectively, I considered,
when once I had got them all stationed—in the very
large, square entrance hall of Dumbarton Grange. And
above the mantelpiece of this hall, showed discreetly
aglow an extensive and a multitudinously colored and
quartered coat of arms within an escutcheon which commemorated my wife's ancestors. It was, when I had
finished it, an heraldic masterpiece which I signed
with complacence.

And gradually we embellished Dumbarton Grange
with yet other fairly ancient heirlooms, as I was given
them or as I purchased them among my wife's so many
soft-voiced relatives in Charles City.

From our dining room, for one instance, we removed
its main feature, in the form of a livid-hued oil painting
depicting a bunch of uncommonly dead-looking mis-
cellaneous fish, for Mr. Shepherd had been what I have
seen described as an ardent fisherman, in favor of an
eighteen-thirtyish large gilt girandole mirror acquired
from the Majors of Burlington. And in the drawing
room, from huge and rigid, olive-green Spanish Mission
chairs, with a supremely uncomfortable sofa to match
them—a sofa which I pronounced to have been designed by the Spanish Inquisition—we relapsed into out-
of-date rosewood chairs and ottomans and still other
time-mellowed Waddill furnishments such as once

might have graced Balmoral, during Prince Albert's heyday.

Our stage setting, in brief, became notable. Always I rejoiced in making more many its knickknacks. And I esteemed it well suited to my wife, who, as I used to mention negligently, was born a Bradley, one of the Charles City Bradleys, the Bradleys of Auburn.

Everybody knew, I would add in tones of apology, how much junk of this sort accumulated in our older Virginian families. And you did not like, it in fact did not seem exactly respectful, just to throw it away.

I was thus painstakingly depreciative because, in the Richmond of 1913, a wife shared socially her husband's rank, by and large, with some indefinable reservations. If she, in fine, were not quite, well, just not quite, why, then there you were! And you stayed there.

The Cabells, it was allowed indulgently, and no matter what brawls and divorces and dark rumors they might have been mixed up in ever since before Richmond was founded, just like the Byrds and the Randolphs and the Lees and the Tuckers, when you came to think about it, still, the Cabells were one of those old families. And those old families were what you might, like the darkies, call quality.

But I remembered that a striking number of these old families' current wives—each one of whom through an odd coincidence had possessed before her marriage an impressive amount of money—had been adjudged to be, well, just not quite. And so in the Richmond

of 1913 these discredited women were allowed to roll in
their wealth unnoticed. No one of them was called
quality. They could not hope ever to get into the
Woman's Club.

My wife nowadays was entitled to the inestimable
honor of attending the Richmond German, because my
own father had been—forgivably, I trust—one of the
founders of that depressing institution. And at the time
of my wife's second marriage, in faraway 1913, there
was no other eminence in Richmond which could pretend to rival, howsoever remotely, a membership in the
Richmond German Club. It was superior even to being
a Colonial Dame, or a member of the Society of the
Cincinnati, during that fantastic era when the upper
classes of Richmond as yet stayed so narrow-minded as
to remain gentry.

And in Charles City County my wife, as young Percie Bradley, had figured as a daughter of the local aris-
tocracy, with what custom termed "the very best people"
her kin and her daily associates. Yet in Richmond, for
all of twelve years, she had been—with a remoteness not
merely geographic—"Mrs. Shepherd out at Dumbarton."

The Shepherd family (from Fluvanna County by
origin), a number of whom I now came to meet and
to admire with sincerity, were sedate and thrifty and all-
meritorious Baptists, concerning whom no rumor had
ever muttered any derogation. Mr. Emmett A. Shepherd alone, and without anybody's putting up with

any nonsense as to his merely personal religious beliefs, so do I suspect, had been converted to the Episcopalian faith. In Charles City County just simply nobody, except colored people of course, was a Baptist. Everybody you knew, or that you ever heard of, was an Episcopalian. So there was not any least bit of sense in this world, Mr. Shepherd, for you to be hardheaded about it.

Such at any rate is my theoretic reconstruction of the past. And in support of my hypothesis I recall the fact, the so very far from irrelevant fact, that during the spring after my marriage I, too, became a communicant of the Protestant Episcopal Church in the United States of America.

Yet the Shepherds, in addition to being thus enviable upon account of their spotless repute, were, as Richmond phrased it, "not anybody in particular." They were persons whom you encountered affably in this or in the other business transaction; but not otherwise. And in consequence—since I never needed to buy any lumber—during the twenty years or thereabouts that my wife and I had both lived in Richmond, at no time had I seen or heard of this Mrs. Shepherd out at Dumbarton until, in the way I have told about, we met each other by chance at the Rockbridge Alum.

Now, hereabouts, of an undertone of snobbishness I become fully aware. So I am not denying that Richmond—in 1913, I mean, of course—was snobbish; nor that, more or less anyhow, I was a by-product of Richmond. My point is merely that inasmuch as the two of us intended to live in Dumbarton, which was a suburb

of Richmond, I thought it wisdom, during my first outlining of Priscilla Bradley Cabell, for the benefit of all
them who were anybody in particular, to respect the
foibles of Richmond.

6

Reverts to Eras Still More Antique

So THEN did I create Priscilla Bradley Cabell, along with Dumbarton Grange. And I likewise proved that life mimics art, through my firm continuance in imitating the conduct of Colonel Rudolph Musgrave immediately after his own marriage, in a story called *The Rivet in Grandfather's Neck*—a book which I had finished writing in 1911, but in 1914 was still unable to get published.

I continued, I mean, just as he did, to search out my wife's ancestry. I pursued with a large painstaking her ancestry, in the combined light of what her kinspeople could tell me about it and of such records as survived of Charles City and the adjoining counties. Resolutely I fared through the back files of the *Virginia Magazine of History and Biography* and of the *William and Mary College Quarterly,* thence entering into *Burke's Peerage* and a not inconsiderable number of the Publications of the Harleian Society. For, still like Colonel

Rudolph Musgrave, I had always enjoyed doing genealogical work; and in this instance, throughout a major
portion of 1914 and of 1915, most richly were my
labors being rewarded.

Nobody in Charles City, so far as I could detect,
had ever done anything in particular during the last
forty-nine years beyond enough desultory farming to
supply one's household with food and clothing. When
General Lee surrendered at Appomattox, then all the
surviving Confederates from Charles City, so it appeared, had returned to their ancestral homes in order
to rest up sort of, and to discuss The War, not unthor-
oughly, for the remainder of their lives.

And this a large number of them were still doing at
the time when I began my research work as to the
Bradleys' and the Waddills' begetters, because a great
many of these veterans had retired from the disbanded
Army of Northern Virginia in their early twenties, and
some of them in their teens. Their wives and their offspring had well learned how to imitate these so un-
hurriedly garrulous ex-Confederates quite docilely,
while everybody sort of rested up after The War. So
what it came to, in 1914, was that no member of the
better families of Charles City seemed ever to do anything except talk about The War—with several of the
more frankly gray-haired ladies becoming eloquent as
to how they had refugeed during The War—or even
ever to have thought about doing anything else, since
the afternoon of 9 April 1865.

But prior to that tragedy the people of Mr. Hill Montague's former typist had been plantation owners, with any number of slaves to attend them. The Bradleys and the Waddills and her ancestors in yet other various "lines," so I found, had served as officers in every American war since the first Indian wars. They had been justices of the peace, and sheriffs, and Quaker ministers of the gospel, and county clerks—here to recall a few of their avatars—and burgesses, and Speakers of the House, and Members of the Governor's Council. They had been Treasurers of the Colony of Virginia, and Surveyors General, and Cape Merchants, and Escheators General, and pretty much everything else conceivable in the form of local prominence. Their daughters had intermarried with three Governors of the Colony of Virginia and with one Governor of the Colony of Albemarle, before ever Albemarle had become North Carolina.

Yes, and the begetters of Mr. Emmett A. Shepherd's aforetime widow traced back into England, repeatedly, beyond question, and in one most gratifying "line" by way of the twelfth son of a perfectly authentic sixteenth-century baron. They descended, with all the needed data to prove it, from at least ten of the peerage who were among the twenty-five sureties for Magna Carta—as well as, for that matter, from King John Lackland likewise. Their ancestry, now that I traced out its never so many origins, included in fact virtually every monarch who had ever reigned anywhere prior to the year of grace 1300.

And indeed, through the Kings of Ireland—upon account of the marriage of Prince Herremon of the Scarlet Thread with a daughter of King Zedekiah of Judah —the direct descent of Priscilla Bradley Cabell stayed a matter of attested and official record as far back as to Adam and Eve, through one hundred and fifty-three generations, to be precise about it.

Here, in short, was a fantastic fine host of such genealogical frippery as could not but bedazzle an authentic Virginian. So I got together an account of fifteen thus far unchronicled Charles City County families, from all whom Priscilla Bradley Cabell was descended. And I made of the not unimpressive result a volume which, upon reflection, I called *The Majors and Their Marriages*.

For my wife's grandmother, the one who married a Waddill, had been before that ceremony Rebecca Priscilla Major. My wife was named after her; and Grandmother Waddill had suffered quite dreadfully from rheumatism. She just sat in a chair all the time you knew her.

But our portrait of her, as a young woman, regarded you with exactly the large and bright and kindly dark eyes which now, incredibly, confronted me every morning at breakfast. Her plentiful, dark hair—which, after having been parted in the middle, had then been brushed down upon both sides far too severely and too sleekly—showed brown with gold in it. My wife, in fact, was the living spit and image of her Grandmother

Waddill, so everybody said in Charles City, before she had rheumatism of course.

"But that," I protested, "that is a rather ill-advised colloquialism, in that it tends to mislead its hearers. And I do wish you would not use it thus dishonestly. You see, it really belongs to Charles City, rather than to Dumbarton Grange."

Whereupon Priscilla Bradley Cabell patted my left cheek and replied affably:—

"You kiss my foot! I know how to talk quite well enough. And I am not going to be bossed by any man alive."

Most certainly, now that I had been married to her for a full year, I was not inclined to dispute this truism. So I said only that outside Charles City no gentlewoman would ever request anybody to kiss her foot. And my wife answered that some people were just naturally born fussycats.

With these points settled, I returned—tacitly—to my handling of the Majors of Burlington as the main theme of my book, with all the other "lines" brought in as collaterals. I had the book printed privately, finishing this process during the December of 1915; and I distributed a fair number of copies among the living descendants of the fifteen families which this book commemorated. But a far larger number of *The Majors and Their Marriages* I presented gratis to the public libraries and to the leading genealogical experts and to the historical societies of the United States in general, but of Virginia in particular. And there, for about seven or six years, the matter rested.

Meanwhile this book had been appraised favorably enough, in a number of historical quarterlies, as an acceptable addition to Virginiana. In Virginia it had been reviewed at gratifying length, and with a bland flavor of encomia, alike in the *William and Mary College Quarterly,* and in the *Virginia Magazine of History and Biography,* and in all three of the Richmond newspapers, during that remote December of 1915. And everybody—or as Richmond discriminated, everybody who counted—was now aware that the quondam Mrs. Shepherd out at Dumbarton "belonged to," as Richmond was accustomed to put it vaguely, "one of those old families."

That mattered a very great deal in Richmond during those far-off days when, with a bridal chorus of backbiting, President Wilson had but lately married Mrs. Norman Galt—"who, after all, was a Bolling," so we granted locally—and when the United States Supreme Court was busied in considering whether or not an income tax would be constitutional.

So then did my fond labors contribute toward shaping yet another aspect of Priscilla Bradley Cabell.

7

Touches Her Dealings with Children

I REMEMBER it was at this period—but about four months earlier, when *The Majors and Their Marriages* was yet in preparation—that we spent quite pleasantly an evening at an informal entertainment given by the Langhorne Putneys, who lived within three miles of us, out at Ruthland.

Priscilla Bradley Cabell, in her customary all-competent manner, drove the car and me back home toward midnight, and she got it into the garage while I hovered about futilely. I did help her close the garage door, however. I very often aided her that much. And after that the two of us went into Dumbarton Grange quietly, so as not to disturb the children.

She then made sure that everything was perfectly all right with Isabelle and with Virginia and with small Emmett also. It had seemed wise at this period to permit her two other children to visit their aunt in Garden City.

I remember likewise how, at near one o'clock in the morning, we were preparing for bed, and how between yawns we were talking about this or the other escapade of Mr. Putney's youth, when she told me:—

"But I am sick. I must have the doctor."

"Hearing," I replied, "is obedience."

I was a little frightened, though.

Then I attended to some rather impassioned telephoning, as a result of which both Dr. Baughman and a colored nurse reached Dumbarton Grange as quickly as could be managed; and in fact they both arrived in fair time to assist in my wife's delivery of a son, at precisely a quarter to two in the morning of the twenty-fifth of August 1915.

I helped them so far as I could. During the worst of it she held both my hands very tightly, I remember. She moaned somewhat. But she did not cry out at all. She was too brave to do that, I was thinking with a delighted admiration, for never had I known my wife to show fear of anything.

However, as I told her a little while later, and I spoke with much painstaking flippancy, because I was still troubled to think about how fond I had become of Priscilla Bradley Cabell, however, when a woman has had five children already, she ought to be used to it. And certainly she had not wasted any time in producing Ballard Hartwell Cabell.

He but narrowly had missed coming to the Putneys' party uninvited, I added. And, although such intrusions might be condoned and passed over without comment

in Charles City County, where expectant mothers by
ordinary chased cows out of the front yard—

In brief, I talked balderdash because I was still very
much upset emotionally.

To which nonsense a forespent and wan-looking but,
nevertheless, a victorious-looking woman answered hap-
pily:

"And what a sweet mouth he has! Oh, but, my dear,
but isn't he just simply the most beautiful thing that
anybody ever saw!"

Well, at bottom I considered that this bluish-colored,
bald-headed, mewing small monster was not anything
of the sort. But I also considered I had better not argue
the matter, not at the moment. One needs to honor the
correct paternal sentiments.

So, without speaking, I kissed my wife upon the
forehead. I kissed her lips. And I consoled myself by
reflecting that, for aught I knew to the contrary, all
newly born babies might look rather like this Ballard
Hartwell Cabell.

It was the name we had picked out a month or so
earlier, because two of my wife's "lines" were the Bal-
lards of York County and the Hartwells of James City.
The name rang, to my hearing, nobly. This name
would fit either a boy or a girl. And so *The Majors and
Their Marriages* was going to be dedicated to him, or
perhaps it might be to her. And it was.

In this manner did Priscilla Bradley Cabell now have
six children to "look after"; and I know that in private

she regarded me as being yet another one of them. It puzzled her to observe my persistence in writing books which nobody in Richmond ever thought of wasting any time on, and which, for that matter, nobody in New York seemed especially eager to publish. Yet if I really wanted to write books, the woman meant to indulge me.

So she did. She almost always did indulge me, finally. Anything which of my own accord I suggested doing, she needed first of course to denounce, with an affable firmness, as being simply the most foolish thing that anybody ever heard of in their born days and completely out of the question. But after this formality had been attended to, and the inferiority of my judgment was established, then without talking any more about the matter, she would fall in with that which I had suggested. For to her it seemed natural, and it, after all, was not wicked, for an intelligent woman to be humoring yet again the least rational of the children under her supervision.

So I was permitted to have all to myself the library upstairs, which was lighted by the same three windows that eventually got into Don Manuel's castle at Storisende. And nobody upon any pretext was allowed to disturb me while I was writing books.

Immediately after breakfast, when the Shepherd children were packed off to their schools and kindergartens, just so was I packed off to the library to write books until lunch time. After lunch I returned to the library, and there, for an hour or two hours, I typed out yet a little more of *The Cream of the Jest,* or as I then called it, *In the Flesh.* Meanwhile, and all day long, that intrepid woman who had married me would be about her own activities, which were numerous and varied and incessant and, to me, for the most part incomprehensible.

She saw to the housekeeping; she supervised the farming; she drove the car into Richmond and back again some three or four times a day so as to attend to the family's requirements in general. We maintained a chauffeur, so far as I could judge, simply in the event of an emergency; for Priscilla Bradley Cabell preferred to do her own driving, thank you, without having anybody else forever putting his mouth in. It followed that the lives of our various chauffeurs at this period were sedentary and immured.

Moreover, the woman had a talent, or to put it more fairly, she had a genius for cooking such as she delighted to display; so she was constantly in and about the kitchen. She conferred with carpenters and plumbers and paper hangers at need; she supervised the seasonal changing of our rugs and window curtains; she arranged about the laundry; she seemed always to be telephoning in regard to this or that or the other affair which demanded to be seen about right away.

She in brief did I know not what: but she managed everything while I wrote books undisturbed in the library upstairs.

And it is my belief that no other human being has ever rested so rarely, or so rarely appeared to need any rest, as did my wife. I do not mean to suggest any element of the tumultuous, but merely that she equably and continuously was at no moment during any day not employed. There was always something which but simply had to be attended to, and right away too, by Priscilla Bradley Cabell in person. So she did attend to it, with an all-friendly and all-overriding competence, while I wrote undisturbed in the library upstairs.

Yet in the evening she was not tired. She, to the contrary, would have liked, I believe, either to go to a party somewhere every evening, or better still, to be giving a party every evening. And I, who did not in the least desire to do these things, I obeyed her complaisantly. At her behest I endured all sorts of social gaieties, evening after evening, in those days. It, I daresay, was good for me; and at any rate, I admired most cordially, even when I did not dream of emulating, her not ever tiring friendliness toward everybody, her quite frank pleasure just in meeting people and talking with them, her endless energy.

Nor did it do me any permanent harm, I think, to attend divine worship at eleven o'clock every Sunday morning, as we were accustomed to do in those days, now that both of us were members of Emmanuel Church—or of "the little Church in the Woods," as the vestry advertised it in the Saturday afternoon papers—over at Brook Hill, within a few miles of Dumbarton Grange.

Mr. Shepherd was buried there, with a Masonic emblem prominent on his foot stone, just back of the church. So after morning services we used to inspect my predecessor's grave every Sunday; she very often placed flowers upon it while I stood by and waited for her to arrange them, feeling slightly awkward; and we were able to keep his section in perfect condition, because Mrs. Joseph V. Johnston and Mrs. James Branch Cabell were the "Grounds Committee" of Emmanuel Church.

With the aid of Old Lucius (as our sexton was called), these two ladies saw to it that the entire cemetery was kept always and everywhere in far more than apple pie order. It was a rather huge cemetery, too, because, in addition to those of our fellow communicants who had died during the last fifty years, it contained likewise a half-regiment or thereabouts of Confederate soldiers killed during the defence of Richmond in 1865.

Priscilla Bradley Cabell took no little pride in the appearance of this trim graveyard which she managed, just at odd moments among her other activities, very much as she managed me, with a benevolent and unsparing competence.

8

She Enters, and Disposes of, Books

MEANWHILE, after having written about her in "A Brown Woman," I continued to write about her. I seem, after our marriage, to have written no book into which she did not enter to some degree.

In the book that I dedicated to her formally she had no part. That was because I had completed *The Rivet in Grandfather's Neck* during the year before the summer in which I encountered Mrs. Emmett A. Shepherd. But in *The Cream of the Jest,* which was the first novel I finished after our marriage, I find her—or to be accurate, I find that already somewhat different phenomenon, Priscilla Bradley Cabell—contributing rather liberally to Kathleen Kennaston, just as in *Jurgen* my wife contributed alike, with a fine impartialness, to Dame Lisa and Chloris and Anaïtis, and still later, to both Niafer and Freydis in *Figures of Earth.*

There is not much of her, I believe, in *The High Place,* wherein I recopied Melior from the original of

42

Mr. Townsend's mother in *The Cords of Vanity;* and wherein Marie Claire was adapted from the original of Bettie Hamlyn in the same story. But into *The Silver Stallion* this Priscilla Bradley Cabell enters under at least three aliases. And always, after that, the protagonist in each of my books of fiction continued to marry somebody who was more or less like her.

It was sheer loving-kindness on my part, it was a vicarious philanthropy, I suppose. I could not imagine any more desirable fate than to be married to a woman who resembled her. And for this reason I inclined always, with a great-hearted generousness, to allot to my protagonist this all-satisfying fate, throughout the entire long list of my short stories and romances, even down to the very last one of them, *The Devil's Own Dear Son.*

At any rate, in this final bit of fiction, I perceive that Mrs. Catherine M. Smith at all times faced life with an alert air of being ready to dispose of any such circumstances as might be foolhardy enough to let her cope with them. And that was my so very efficient wife, I know, as she herself would have phrased it, just all over.

I do not think that she detected this so constant portrayal, not quite of her exactly, but of her this or the other trick of speech, or it might be some trait of hers, in which I had rejoiced. I do not think that she ever, or at least not precisely, read through any one of my books.

Whensoever I published a book, then resolutely she would take a copy of it to bed with her; and she would read some of it with a resigned and persevering politeness, while from my own adjoining bed I pretended not to be watching her. But upon all such occasions she would put by the book before very long; without speaking, she would turn over toward the north so as to get out of her eyes the glare from the reading light which stood between our beds; and somewhat earlier than usual, she would go to sleep.

The affair terminated thus tacitly. Afterward she did not ever comment upon the book, either to commend or to disapprove of it. But her silence had an indefinable flavor of dismissing with tact an affair which, after all, was not worth talking about.

She, in brief, was no whit interested in books. She defended untiringly, jealously and fiercely that occlusion in the library upstairs which I needed in order to write books. When anybody spoke in praise of my books it pleased her. She at once regarded that person with approval and fondness. She beamed visibly upon any such civil and considerate and surprising person with an enthusiasm which I found to be embarrassing.

Yet at bottom, I know, she still thought that to be writing or to be reading books was a rather shiftless waste of time when there were so many important things which but simply had to be attended to, and right off too, such as having the car washed, or putting up your jellies and your blackberry wine and your preserves, or fetching a man out to tune the piano, or ask-

ing in a few people for dinner, or conferring with Miss
Talcott, or Miss Jennie Ellett as to the progress of your
children at school, or seeing to it that your furnace was
overhauled for the winter, or making sure that Old
Lucius really did get every one of those fallen tree limbs
out of Emmanuel cemetery before Sunday.

And in addition to these imperative matters, as time
went by, then time evoked yet other affairs which but
just simply had to be attended to, at a considerably farther distance from Dumbarton Grange, in spite of my
occasional mild protests.

Because, my darling, thus would Priscilla Bradley
Cabell explain to me aloofly, when you had three growing daughters, who else was going to see to it that they
got the proper advantages and went with the right sort
of people? It was a matter of plain duty for any mother
anywhere.

So as my various stepdaughters, Priscilla Shepherd
and Grace Shepherd and Virginia Shepherd, became
older, and as they began severally to attend various
boarding schools in the North, and to attend likewise
the dances and the gaieties of commencement time at
the University of Virginia, and at the Virginia Military
Institute, and at Annapolis, and at West Point, then
Priscilla Bradley Cabell remained utterly adamantean
as to the fact that she chaperoned her daughters at every
one of these festivities merely because it was her plain
duty to do so.

And at such times, I think, she believed what she

was saying. The delighted interest which she got out of observing and of thus sharing in her children's career as college belles (in which role they were each rather unusually successful) this long-suffering yet steadfast woman elected to class as an irrelevant by-product of performing her plain duty. She was equally firm when it came to her daughters', one by one, making their debuts, and thus entering formally into the accepted social circles of Richmond and meeting the people that counted.

She attended to these matters just simply and solely because to look after things like that was her plain duty. She told me so herself. And if, in the line of duty, she was thus forced to take part in, or to act as hostess at, a fairly vast number of dinners and teas and luncheons and dances and still other forms of what I, meekly attendant thereupon, esteemed to be highly tedious nuisances, she at least did not flinch.

So consummate was this duty's martyr's acting's perfection that you would have thought she was enjoying herself whole-heartedly. So strong was her will-power that she stayed on until the very end of every one of these pernicious affairs, what while I fidgeted and yawned, or lurking morosely, whether in our own hallway or in somebody else's hallway, smoked unconsoling cigarettes.

9

Culminates Strangely, with a Cross

MOREOVER, she became interested in patriotic matters. This did not happen until an excess of eight years after our marriage, when, with all the children, except Ballard and Isabelle off at school, she could find spare time for the social aspects of patriotism.

It was then out of a clear sky, as people say (with an article about it in each of the Richmond papers), that Mrs. James Branch Cabell established the Pocahontas Chapter of Daughters of the American Colonists, the first group of this order in Virginia; and she was chosen to head this group under the impressive title of Virginia State Regent. Here *The Majors and Their Marriages*, which was now a reference book to be found in all state libraries and most genealogical libraries, came rather nobly into play, because it showed that Priscilla Bradley Cabell had virtually every known sort of "Colonial claim."

And besides that, this woman who was friendly with

47

everybody, was liked even by the intimidating, large, acidulous ladies who wore enamelled bright badges and conducted similar patriotic societies—mainly, so did I infer, through blackballing all members of their sex who were not quite. As to the quiteness of Mrs. James Branch Cabell of Dumbarton Grange, however, they concurred beamingly.

What followed was that before long I found myself married to not merely a Daughter of the American Colonists, but also to a Daughter of the American Revolution, and to a Member of the First Families of Virginia, and to a Colonial Dame of America, and to a Daughter of the Colonial Wars, and to a Member of the Order of the Crown, and to a Descendant of Knights of the Garter, and to a Daughter of the Barons of Runnemede, and to a Daughter of the Seventeenth Century likewise. I believe that includes all the efficient, brown-haired patriots added to my harem eventually, even though there may well have been several others. I lost count after a while.

Every April each one of them would go on to Washington, where these descendants and members and dames and daughters devoted a full week to attending the Annual Meetings of the societies to which each belonged. Whatever was accomplished at these Annual Meetings I never quite understood. But I do very well know that, with an edifying gravity, Priscilla Bradley Cabell enjoyed every one of her Annual Meetings. She, in fact, thought it was just simply a matter of plain duty for the members of a society to show their interest in that society by attending its Annual Meeting.

She explained to me this circumstance every April, immediately prior to leaving me for Washington. And if, here again, the performnce of her plain duty entailed taking part in a great many luncheons and dinner parties, and resulted in her being thrown with all sorts of people that it was real interesting to talk to—such as Miss Anne Morgan and President Hoover and Mr. Samuel P. Gompers, I remember at random—why, but here again, Priscilla Bradley Cabell did not ever flinch.

And in the majestic role of Virginia State Regent she ordained for the Pocahontas Chapter of Daughters of the American Colonists an employment rather different from the severe blackballing of all such petticoated persons as were not quite.

For there was, so the untiring woman had found out somewhere, a process, by me uncomprehended, through which a time-scarred and decrepit manuscript volume may be "restored" and made as hale as ever it seemed when newly written. And as I had told her while working on *The Majors and Their Marriages*, a great number of our more ancient and valuable Virginian county record books were time-dilapidated beyond handling. So they had to be kept locked up; they could not be consulted; and they were thus rendered useless.

Which was, so did Priscilla Bradley Cabell decide, just plain out-and-out nonsense such as nobody anywhere ought to have any least bit of patience with.

The fruit of this decision was that her personally conducted chapter of Daughters of the American Colonists at once raised sufficient funds and "restored" therewith one of these record books, in I forget nowadays what county; during the following year they repeated this sequence; and always after that they "restored" yet another county record book annually. These books were thus restored to circulation also. They were made accessible to genealogists and to students of Virginian history.

Here then at last was a patriotic society engaged in work of some actual and unarguable consequence. So the Colonial Dames of America in the State of Virginia now emulated the Pocahontas Chapter of Daughters of the American Colonists, by "restoring" a book of age-damaged Virginian records. Then yet another chapter of the daughters or the descendants of something or other did the same thing.

And steadily the beneficent virus of "restoring" spread. By-and-by you could find in the state of Virginia hardly any group of embadged patriots, whether female or masculine, who were not "restoring" a book of Virginian records. And it was Priscilla Bradley Cabell who had led them into doing something of rather large importance, now that, instead of being scattered throughout the state and locked up in the safes of various county court houses, all these "restored" records were assembled at Richmond, in a special room of the Virginia State Library, where anybody who wished to consult them could do so with entire convenience.

She arranged about this housing problem also, after having shared in a few friendly conferences with Dr. Henry R. McIlwaine, who was then our Virginia State Librarian. He was a real nice old gentleman, she reported, after you had once told him just exactly what he had to do next, and without any more shilly-shallying about it either.

Yet furthermore, it was she who induced—and who perhaps nagged, or cajoled, or even bullyragged, during the long while, of at least eleven years, which her task demanded—she induced somehow, at any rate, the National Society of Daughters of the American Colonists to erect that wholly handsome huge memorial, in the form of a stone cross, which nowadays marks the spot, at Cape Henry in Virginia, where the first permanent English settlers landed in the April of 1607.

Mrs. James Branch Cabell, with an article about it in all the Richmond papers, unveiled this memorial to her pertinacity in the April of 1935. And always afterward her delight in that cross stayed unbridled. With an unhidden pride, the woman believed it was this cross which had justified her existence upon earth. I cannot think with any calm about her illogic when I remember what her existence did actually mean, to one of her acquaintances, forever and at every moment after the summer of 1912.

10

Concerns Patriotism and Pygmalion

However! if when once her hand was in, she did join a rather surprising number of hereditary patriotic societies, I admit that I abetted, I even encouraged her, in the acquiring of these harmless honorifics; because, after all, it was I who had unearthed and who had catalogued her prodigious ancestry.

So it was always with a somewhat Pygmalion-like feeling that I filled out the application papers and supplied the data which would enable her to enter into yet another one of these impressive incarnations. But for me, I reflected, she would never have been any of these descendants and dames and daughters, whom I had, in a sense, created.

She very much enjoyed being them. She, in particular, enjoyed being Virginia State Regent for Daughters of the American Colonists. And I found it a marvel to note how, without any least training in such matters, she presided over their meetings, and made small graceful speeches to them, and acquired a working knowledge of what they tell me is called Parliamentary law, with a calm and cordial competence.

Not that I was ever admitted to these gatherings. But when the Daughters met, as was ordinarily the case, at their Regent's home, with an informal luncheon afterward, then I used to sit upon the hall stairway outside, whence I could listen with approval to the earnest voice of Priscilla Bradley Cabell speaking, speaking never so tranquilly and with a quiet friendliness, to the assembled gentlewomen in her quaint drawing room.

I glowed then with calm pride in her. There, in fact, seems no harm in my admitting bluntly that even after several years of marriage, I was still interested by this woman.

And in part, my interest was that of an artist who regards his own work with complacence. For if my all-competent wife had refashioned me into a quiet, smoothly running engine which now manufactured books without let or hindrance, and if she had thus made possible all that which, in those remote times, people almost gravely called my literary career, I, too, had changed her.

To begin with, I had converted a Rebecca P. Shepherd into Priscilla Bradley Cabell; and the improvement I thought to be more than nominal. Through my constant and just simply pernickety ways of always fussing about nothing whatever, I had checked the colloquialisms of Charles City so far as went public utterance

In private, they continued to regale me and to enrich my writing; but in all social intercourse, as time passed, Priscilla Bradley Cabell employed fewer and yet fewer of them, as the pedantic say, *coram populo,* because of my being such a continual old fuss-budget.

She had now come to avoid them completely, except only among her nearer intimates. She, as it were, now spoke two languages, interchangeably, every day. And her linguistic dualism was my doing.

It was my doing, likewise, the manner in which she now arranged her beautiful brown hair, so as to cover part of her ears, which were too broad at the top, and so as to form a knot very low down at the back of her so freely and proudly poised head. It was my doing that she wore at all times a necklace of some sort. It was my doing that the Virginia State Regent, in her official capacity, produced an exceedingly large host of manifestoes voiced in a stately and impressive English such as was quite generally commented upon and admired by Daughters of the American Colonists.

Yes, and it was my doing that when she was elected Historian of the Daughters of the Barons of Runnemede, the all-versatile woman produced likewise, for the society's Year Book, a learned and a most edifying treatise about the signing of Magna Carta. Her scholarship surprised me. And it was my doing that she wore this or the other shade of purple almost always. . . .

But I would not seem to boast. In brief, there were nowadays very many multiform small changes made from "Mrs. Shepherd out at Dumbarton," changes upon which I used to reflect pridefully, with a Pygmalion-like feeling.

Our marriage improved both of us, in short; and in chief, because we did not have any traits whatever in common. Here was a deficiency which enabled each to supply for the other very nearly all that which the other lacked. She attended to every practical matter, unquestioned, because she understood about such matters. But to me she relinquished—completely, and shruggingly, and with a flavor of compassion—any affairs which displayed a cultural or aesthetic aspect, because of my being, as concerned these minor features of our shared living, just a perpetual old fuss-budget.

11

Dwells upon Her Genius as a Critic

AND to her unending energy, meanwhile, had been opened yet other fresh fields of exercise when, starting with *The Cream of the Jest,* in 1917, my books began to be read by a few persons here and there, and when after the attempted suppression of *Jurgen,* in 1920, the notion somehow got abroad that I was a writer of ponderable importance.

I, for a while, became, in fact, as I have read with pleasure, "an ideational gonfalon." To the contriver of that phrase I forever shall remain grateful admiringly. I myself found it rather a nuisance being an ideational gonfalon; but Priscilla Bradley Cabell enjoyed it fervently, now that the two of us were becoming acquainted with so very many other writers who, at this period, seemed rather more than ready to answer to the same description. I mean that, in self-esteem at least, pretty much every one of us was an ideational gonfalon in the decreed battle against prudery and the

Puritan, and the *boobus Americanus* in general, over which the 1920's raised their quaint pother.

She was at her quiet and cordial best in meeting and in making friends with and in playing hostess to that exuberant throng of editors and of publishers and of authors and of authoresses whom the 'twenties ranked as pre-eminent. A lot of them seemed right sort of funny, she admitted in private; for in private, as I have said, she still adhered to the colloquialisms of Charles City.

But she got on swimmingly with every one of these large literary figures, even with those among them who seemed right sort of funny; because it remained, when all was said, my wife's unshakable if politely unvoiced opinion that anybody who wrote books, or who talked about books quite seriously, ought not to be regarded as a rational person. And in consequence, with a flavor of maternal pity, she was always especially pleasant in dealing with the sophisticated and flamboyant, world-famous Titans of literature who made glorious the 1920's.

She had not read any of their books, nor did she pretend to have done so. She did not hearten these great writers with any least fraudulence as to intending by-and-by to read their books. And yet they every one of them regarded Priscilla, as they termed her—excepting only Ellen Glasgow, to whom she was Percie—with an unaffected affection. It was a miracle that I could never understand in the light of my knowledge as to the sustaining vanity and the egoism but for which no

one of these writers—including myself, I daresay—
would ever, quite so visibly, have thought either his
or her most recent book to be wholly worth the labor
invested in writing it.

In fact, I sometimes wonder about those so very
transiently pre-eminent and nowadays so antique writers of the 'twenties, about whom I shall need to be
speaking by-and-by, and who to Priscilla Bradley Cabell
in their all-glorious heyday seemed right sort of funny.
And I mean me, too, as to whose underlying childishness, if not exactly my idiocy, she at no time nurtured
any doubt. This always competent woman, in addition
to her other trenchant qualities, may have had the
makings of a sound and far-seeing literary critic, I sometimes reflect, nowadays.

Her first newspaper interview was granted, uncon-
sciously, in the October of 1922, to Burton Rascoe,
whom at the time she had known for some two or three
years; and Burton, somewhat to my confusion, printed
it in the *New York Tribune,* of which he was then the
literary editor.

Mrs. James Branch Cabell (he recorded in his
"Bookman's Day Book") is up from Richmond to see
her children who are at school here. She was in mourn-
ing, and I did not recognize her in the hotel lobby until
Guy Holt called me over. Like most Southern women,
she refers always to her husband as Mr. Cabell, never
calling him James, Jim or Jimmy. . . .

Mrs. Cabell told me that Cabell was "still fussing"

about her choice of a place to take a vacation this year. . . .

"There wasn't anyone we knew in particular going to Virginia Beach this summer, the place where Mr. Cabell wrote most of *Jurgen* and some of his other books, so I decided to go to Mountain Lake instead," my wife explained to Rascoe, without consciousness that, through him, she was addressing the public at large. "Mr. Cabell made an awful fuss about it, and said he couldn't work there. After we came back he said he hadn't been able to do a lick of work all summer; his whole summer had gone to waste; and for me to tell Mr. Holt that his book wasn't even started yet. But I am not going to tell Mr. Holt any lie about it; Mr. Cabell's book is most finished."

Guy Holt, it may be interpolated, was at this period the acting literary editor for my publishers; and about him I shall be speaking later. Meanwhile the book referred to was *The High Place,* which at the time of this interview was some eight long months from being finished.

"On the porch at the beach," Priscilla Bradley Cabell continued, according to Rascoe, "Mr. Cabell had a certain little table he liked to write on, and he complained that the table we got for him in the mountains had one leg that was short, so that the table wobbled, and he couldn't write. I fixed it up by sticking something under the short leg of the table, and I made him comfortable as could be. I always do have to look after him, just like a baby.

"He really is the most helpless human being that you ever saw in your life. And he wrote all right, but grumbling all the time. Now that he is back home, he pretends he hasn't written anything and that I am to blame for it, for taking him to the mountains when he wanted to go to the beach. But I know better. He just likes to be stubborn.

"So I do not pay one bit of attention to him. I just ignore him, and see that he has everything he wants, and I keep people away from him. He doesn't like it now because I am up here in New York; and he keeps writing that he can't do any work because he has to answer the telephone all the time. Of course, when I am home, I answer the phone for him; and I tell people he is not there when he doesn't want to see them. So he really wants me to hurry back because he likes to have me to wait on him."

And she said yet furthermore, still to be quoting from Burton Rascoe:—

"A little wait won't hurt him. He has made me wait enough times. Why, but do you know what he does time and again, when I tell him we are going out somewhere to a party? and he says all right, but after I get ready and come downstairs, I find him not dressed and declaring up and down that he hadn't heard anything about our going out and refusing absolutely to budge. So then I just go on without him."

Being human, I did not wholly relish this seeming monologue when I first encountered it in print. There

were far too many truths in it, I felt, fidgeting somewhat, for it to be included in a newspaper's book section.

But today I reflect that Rascoe showed an acute ear.
He caught almost exactly the colloquial style of Charles
City County, which Priscilla Bradley Cabell retained
always among her intimates, and with Burton Rascoe
and Guy Holt we were both intimate in those days. She
did not know she was being interviewed.

Otherwise, she would have remembered less vocally
my making an awful fuss over an alleged inability to
do a lick of work and my general domestic status as the
most helpless human being that you ever saw in your
life, just like a baby. She would have employed, instead, the rather more formal English, befitting—and
nowadays habitual to—a Virginia State Regent.

12

Her Deeds and Duties in the 1920's

S HE had a talent for living, and got such joy out of it." That was, it may be recalled, my first impression of her. And it is a summary which I think to be wholly just when I remember the twelve years we spent at Dumbarton Grange. With a tinge of surprise, I now note how infrequently, throughout these same twelve years, the two of us were ever left alone together between breakfast and bedtime, what with my continual writing in the library upstairs, and what with her having to manage, zestfully, and with vigor, and completely, so very many other matters besides a husband.

Those years, when I look back upon them, seem to have passed with a strange swiftness. They have taken on, nowadays, a dreamlike quality. I find in them a bright-tinted, alien unreality. I feel, nowadays, that it was not I but a far different and how far more complacent person who lived through those brisk and busy, so very well contented years.

Then Isabelle Shepherd died, and Priscilla Shep-

herd had married. And Grace Shepherd and Virginia
Shepherd both were about to be married; and Emmett
A. Shepherd, Jr., was at work in remote Texas; and
Priscilla Bradley Cabell had decided to move into Richmond. Because, my darling, so did she explain with an
emphatic patience, Dumbarton Grange was entirely too
large for the two of us and Ballard to be staying on here
by ourselves.

Moreover (it was mentioned), I ought to have some
rays of common sense about servants. They simply
would not consent to live this far out in the country,
not nowadays, unless you paid them perfectly ridiculous
prices and gave them their own private automobile to
ride in town every night. That the speaker had not any
patience whatever with their nonsense was a fact dwelt
upon with a continuance in emphasis. It was enough to
drive anybody crazy. Because what in the world could
you do about it? You were right at their mercy every
minute. You were utterly and entirely and completely
helpless. You did not dare to say one single word.

So I did not dare to say one single word.

It followed that we disposed of Dumbarton Grange,
and in 1925 we moved into Richmond, where she had
found upon Monument Avenue a house which would
suit quite well with some repapering. Optimism spoke
there, as we both conceded, later on, perforce. And at
3201 Monument Avenue she allotted to me yet another library upstairs wherein to write books.

Well, but in Richmond she continued to enjoy life

hugeously, now that every evening, when there was not a party somewhere, she could so easily visit some of her friends, or at the very least have three of her friends come in to play bridge. There were beginning to be grandchildren: that afforded her yet something else to attend to. Then intermittently and constantly there would be editors or authors or publishers coming to Richmond whom we really ought to have in, along with Ellen Glasgow and perhaps a reporter from the *Times-Dispatch*, just for cocktails at any rate, as a matter of plain duty.

And, besides that, there were trips to New York in connection with my books. Priscilla Bradley Cabell delighted in going to New York, and in holding high revel there with its then current literati. But always all such outings had to be understood, quite definitely, as being just for my own good and a matter of plain duty. More often than not, she would esteem it needful to point out how very extremely inconvenient she was finding her plain duty to go to New York at this special time.

And now and then while we were in New York, during the days of my famousness, she used to be interviewed. She liked being interviewed, I believe. And for my part, I admired at any rate one interview with her which appeared early in 1932.

I found it, and I still find it, to be sound portraiture; and for that reason I am citing some of it, omitting only

those passages which dealt with my complete dependence upon her, or which stressed—as I considered,
rather too vividly—my persistent pig-headedness.

"I am my husband's secretary and his chauffeur, and
I don't know what else I can say besides that," began
Mrs. James Branch Cabell. But . . . as she defined the
duties of "secretary" and "chauffeur" to the somewhat
eccentric writing man who is her husband, these two
jobs turned out to be very different from the ordinary
versions of them. . . .

Behind the musical slurrings and elisions of her Virginia speech there emerged a picture of an author's wife
who is what you think an author's wife should be.
When her husband retires into his study to work she
stands like a wall between him and disturbance, firmly
turning away ladies who come from California bearing
a book to be autographed and gentlemen who put their
foot inside the door and protest that Mr. Cabell has
agreed to look at their manuscript this morning. She
turns down invitations for him, takes him home from
parties when he shows the first signs of fatigue, and
graciously pours the cocktails at his literary afternoons.

And there is a slight suspicion that, although she
would never dream of saying so, she looks upon the
world of fancy in which her husband spends his days
as a little—oh, ever so little—touched with madness.
Perhaps the interviewer was mistaken, but there seemed
to be something derisive about the look in Mrs. Cabell's

eyes—which are of an almost tawny brown—and in the curve of her lips as she said:—

"James is a perfectly normal man until after he has had his breakfast coffee and opened his mail. Then he goes upstairs, into his library, to write his books." . . .

Nor is she jealous of that witch woman who, as Mr. Cabell has pointed out in *Beyond Life,* is never a man's wife, and who in the guise of Helen, or some other lovely wraith, haunts the dreams of all men, including Mr. Cabell.

"That woman is only a woman in a book," Mrs. Cabell pointed out, "and it never occurred to me to be jealous of anybody on paper. I have never known a jealous moment since I married James."

Mrs. Cabell approves of her husband's books, which she reads, not in manuscript, but as soon as they have been published. "I read them right through and get it over with," she said. . . .

Mrs. Cabell herself is quite the antithesis of a woman in a book. Her life is concerned with such realities as telling persistent telephone callers that Mr. Cabell does not autograph books, and mending Mr. Cabell's clothes, and finding time meanwhile to bring up her five children by her first marriage and her young son, who is also Mr. Cabell's son, as well as giving advice and counsel on the upbringing of her grandchildren, of whom there are now five.

"For James married me when I was a widow with five children—wasn't he brave?" she demanded. . . .

Being a housewife who has raised a family, and is

now helping to raise grandchildren, and is active in various patriotic societies—she is president of the Richmond chapter of the Daughters of American Colonists —is an ideal career for an author's wife, so Mrs. Cabell thinks.

Well, it is questionless that I cannot understand the mention of "mending Mr. Cabell's clothes." For she detested sewing. She never, during my acquaintance with her, did any sewing whatever, nor, I am certain, did she pretend to have done any. But that she did pretend always to take me home from parties when I showed any sign of fatigue, and to have read right straight through every one of my books, I do not doubt. She very often yielded in social converse to these two flights of imagination, and even when I was present.

In brief, I find all that which I have quoted to be a sound enough portraiture of Priscilla Bradley Cabell when she was not speaking, it is noticeable, just as everybody that you ever heard of had always talked in Charles City. She was being interviewed consciously.

And I like in particular her notion as to an ideal career for an author's wife—which was to attend with competence to her own department in our shared living without ever interfering with mine. Her sole interest in my writing was to see to it that, inasmuch as I wanted to write books, I should be permitted to do so unbothered.

She enjoyed, as it were, the role of being my untiring watchdog. She gloried in it. She delighted to talk about it, and to dwell at large, both proudly and fondly, upon how very helpless I would have been without her.

But I did not object in particular. The truth needs to be respected.

13

Tells of How the Ending Commenced

AND then, in those untroubled days, then every summer she enjoyed our two or three months' stay at Mountain Lake, where we had builded Cayford Cottage—with a glass-enclosed small porch-room, for me to write books in—and where, because virtually the same persons returned to Mountain Lake every summer, she had scores of intimate acquaintances with whom to go fishing (in which, precisely as Mr. Shepherd had done, she delighted), or with whom to play bridge (in which likewise she delighted, all-scientifically, in accord with Mr. Culbertson's very latest rulings), or with whom to tramp the wide sprawling hills in a search for mushrooms.

She had come, somehow, to know all about mushrooms. Without hesitating could she distinguish between the edible and the poisonous varieties. It was to her an unfailing joy to wander abroad gathering in a wicker basket all such mushrooms as would not, according to Charles City, kill you dead as a door nail, and then, with the aid of a small electric heater, to cook these mushrooms upon the back porch of Cayford Cottage. After that, she would carry down the hill toward the hotel a sizzling, huge kettleful of them for our supper, in the hotel dining room, sending over by our waiter a liberal portion to the table of this or the other of her special friends, and glowing visibly, with an artist's fond pride, over their enjoyment of her unparalleled cooking.

Yes, very certainly Priscilla Bradley Cabell had a talent for living; and out of every one of these homely, everyday avocations at Mountain Lake she got a constant and companionable contentment.

Moreover, and always, there was the patriotic work, which continued unabated the year round; and which, apart from the annual visits to Washington, demanded, in Richmond also, attendance upon a number of luncheons and tea parties and card parties and dinner parties. You paid for your admission to these entertainments, thus helping to raise funds for the patriotic work of that society which was giving the entertainment. This circumstance converted any pleasure which you might derive from taking part in these entertainments into an incidental feature of performing your plain duty.

All the while, this Priscilla Bradley Cabell stayed slender and young looking and, to my finding, remarkably pretty. Her plentiful, brown hair, now that she

had passed sixty, had not anywhere a touch of gray.
Her face was unfurrowed always, except for that single,
straight up-and-down line in between the top of her
nose and her right eyebrow, that perpendicular very
small furrow which of a sudden came into being upon
her forehead under the stress of mental concentration;
or whenever, as so rarely happened, she was dissatisfied;
or when, perhaps for as long as a half-second, she
stayed uncertain as to what she meant to do next.

Her eyes, her so vividly brown eyes, remained keen
and cordial. Almost always just before she began to
speak she would smile suddenly and brightly. She did
not seem to me to have aged or to have changed in any
feature whatever during the twenty-two years of our
married life. She appeared ageless.

Then toward the midsummer of 1936, without any
warning, in her comely and staunch and nimble and
her never-tiring body, developed Grandmother Waddill's rheumatism. It was, though, what the doctors
nowadays called arthritis. And it became worse and yet
worse, swiftly, unrelentingly, pitilessly, in spite of the
unlimited remedies which doctors had discovered, and
advocated so glibly, for this disease.

We tried them all. Month after month, throughout
a trio of unrewarding years, and in many hospitals, we
tried them. . . .

But I have not the heart to remember this season of
her so multitudinous "treatments." I remember only

that every one of these "treatments" proved ineffective against Grandmother Waddill's rheumatism, which at long last had made impossible for my wife her so cheery and forever active manner of living.

14

Of Divers Adjustments with Destiny

WELL! and so the indomitable woman made the best of it. She was condemned henceforward to live in never ending pain, which varied only by shifting from one part of her body to another part, or by being worse upon some days than it was on others. She found, though, through the final advice of the doctor at Johns Hopkins, when with frankness he dismissed her case as being incurable, that by taking an aspirin tablet every four hours it was possible somewhat to deaden her pain.

She was forever crippled; but at least she could yet walk, howsoever near at times it came to hobbling, for a brief distance, slowly. Her hands had stiffened so that she had not always full control of them; but they still sufficed her, more or less dependably, in driving an automobile.

For, after refusing, with emphasis, to be bothered for one single second longer by any good-for-nothing chauffeur who was always putting his mouth in, the way that every one of them did invariably, she had begun upon all occasions to drive her own car. Driving, now that she was crippled, had become her main pleasure. It enabled her to get about and to see something of her friends, she explained, instead of just staying stuck up in the house all the time. And she remained, as yet, an adroit, skilled, fearless and always careful driver.

Meanwhile, of necessity, we had quit Cayford Cottage, and we had put behind us forever our summers at Mountain Lake, which throughout fifteen years she had enjoyed so heartily, now that a cripple was not able to walk from the cottage to the hotel, or, for that matter, ever again to get up the hill upon which Cayford Cottage stood. And to replace it, we had builded yet another summer home, at the mouth of the Potomac River, in low-lying, level Northumberland County, naming this summer cottage Poynton Lodge, upon account of Priscilla Bradley Cabell's being descended from that aforetime-mentioned sixteenth-century baron, who was one of the Warrens of Poynton, in Cheshire.

And she constructed this eleven-room, two-story dwelling without being aggravated, a great deal more than enough to try the patience of a saint, by any living architect anywhere, with their high-and-mighty notions. She accomplished this task through the forthright process of telling the local carpenters exactly what she did want and just exactly where she wanted it put; and after that, of supervising their labors every day. She improvised and she perfected any number of architectural betterments while the building was in progress. But among her very first requirements, as I recall matters, was a glass-enclosed small porch-room, so that in the summer time Mr. Cabell would have somewhere to write his books.

The carpenters heard and obeyed. So satisfying were the results of their subservience that when Poynton Lodge was finished, I remember, she gave them a party. It took the form of a luncheon, a notably plenteous luncheon, at which mint juleps and Brunswick stew figured in a shared prominence, my wife having rejoicingly allowed our cook a day off in order that she, herself, might compile these refreshments with infirm hands but unfailing art; and throughout which luncheon Priscilla Bradley Cabell, now in her favorite role as hostess, a role which to her own brown eyes seemed preferable even to enacting the part of a cook, enjoyed every moment thoroughly in converse with our four carpenters.

And always after that we spent each summer at Poynton Lodge, quietly and with contentment, among a loyal assemblage of her children and of her grandchildren, for her to be directing, and without putting up with any nonsense either, in all matters whatever, simply for their own good.

But in winter we were compelled to go to Florida

upon account of my kleptomaniac attitude toward pneumonia germs.

It was upon the fourteenth of January in 1935 that in the city of Richmond I developed my first case of pneumonia; and I was taken to Florida to recover from the after effects of my malady in, as the affair fell out, the city of St. Augustine. And there I did recover. But upon the fourteenth of January in 1936 I again had pneumonia; and again I was returned to St. Augustine for recuperation.

So when at nine o'clock in the evening of the fourteenth of January in 1937, I once more was beset, and rather nearly killed out of hand, by pneumonia—of that virulent kind in which the crisis comes first, and with the diffidence of a thunderbolt—why, then reflection suggested that I was getting into a rut and contracting over-expensive habits. How very much more thrifty it would be, reflection rationalized, to go to St. Augustine a while before the fourteenth of next January; and thus, perhaps, to avoid having any pneumonia at all, along with the attendant doctors' bills and nurses' bills and druggists' bills, not here to be thinking untactfully, reflection added, anything about the morticians'.

We honored in 1938 the advice of reflection; and during this year I did not have pneumonia.

I remember, though, that at five o'clock in the afternoon of the fourteenth of January—upon Palm Row in St. Augustine, and in the presence of four witnesses—an unaccounted-for, rather large, although short-legged, brown dog, for no apparent reason, attacked and bit me, silently and severely, just eight inches below my left knee. That was perhaps a coincidence; but I have the scar to show for it; and, in any case, I preferred a dog to pneumonia.

15

Centers Very Largely on Christmas

So THEN did my wife and Ballard and I begin to drive
southward every year as soon after Christmas as could
be managed—and with Priscilla Bradley Cabell regnant
in the driver's seat of our car. Each year she became
more thoroughly crippled; but she was still quite able
to drive the seven hundred and some odd miles between
Richmond and St. Augustine, so did she insist.

She, of course, was not able to do anything of the
sort. It had become, in fact, a complete, plain, physical
impossibility. And for this reason, very often I used to
wonder just how the incredible woman could manage
to do it, nevertheless, with an unperturbed nonchalance.
She did not ever have any particular patience, though,
with an impossibility when it concerned something
about which she had already made up her mind.

Yet before leaving Richmond, it was necessary for
us to be giving a party upon Christmas Day. In Charles

City County, at Christmas, people always did have in their family and just a few friends for eggnog. Or at any rate, everybody that you ever heard of did this. And so we had to do this, too.

The large trouble was that our respect for Charles City's time-hallowed customs entailed a preliminary week of skilled labor in the form of cake making—the products of which needed annually to include a pound cake and a fruit cake and a white-fruit cake and a Japanese fruit cake and a chocolate cake and a fig cake—as well as in the form of baking the ham, and of roasting the turkey, and of making some seven or eight pies, or maybe we had better say an even dozen pies this year, just so as to stay on the safe side. You never knew who might drop in.

Officially, these labors were performed by Lula Kenny, who had cooked for us ever since we were married; but in every one of these labors did Priscilla Bradley Cabell share daily—or perhaps hourly would be more accurate—because there was not any known way of keeping her out of what, after all, and even if you kept on talking yourself black in the face, and sounding crazy as a June bug, was her own kitchen, thank you.

Then upon Christmas Eve she had need to devote an hour or so to preparing the eggnog with a far more than pharmaceutical accuracy. For she compounded this beverage just as everybody that you ever heard of had always made it in Charles City.

I never understood much about the process. But I do

know that first you had to get special cream from the dairy. Later, you whipped up the eggs. And for what seemed to me at least two hours, you at intervals would pour into a huge yellow bowl a very little of this and then of the other. You had to continue stirring it, though, all the time, as cautiously as if you were handling high explosives, and with a small straight up-and-down line on your forehead.

By-and-by you would dribble in just a teeny, wee little bit more of something else; and you kept on stirring and beating up everything. The eggs also—or perhaps it was only the whites of the eggs—had to go in, I believe, thus gradually. Anyhow, I can remember that the cupful of brandy and the nutmeg were the very last things which you added before you stirred it all up yet again, slowly and magisterially, for about two or three more minutes, and before the results were put into our refrigerator, along toward eleven o'clock in the evening, for an overnight stay there.

It followed that upon Christmas morning an eggnog that was really eggnog would be fit for anybody to drink, and not like the stuff most people gave you.

But it followed likewise that, after the week or so of varied labors such as I have indicated, then Priscilla Bradley Cabell upon Christmas Day would feel sort of like the last of pea-time and about completely tuckered out. She would enjoy her party; never in her life did she fail to enjoy a party; but she would share in its gaieties somewhat haggardly. And when Christmas was over and done with, she would have to rest up in bed for a day or two before we could get started for Florida.

Then after she had finished her two days' steady driving to St. Augustine, she yet again would collapse. And so in St. Augustine likewise she would have to rest up in bed before trying to get everything unpacked, and with every bit of the food, when they finally did consent to bring it over to your room, just as cold as a stone.

Yet, furthermore, it followed that I suggested we had better leave Richmond before Christmas, and permit one of my stepchildren to help out with the driving. And after this outrageous notion, of any mother's not spending Christmas Day properly with all her family, had been denounced and stigmatised and rejected and vilipended, with an indignant firmness, as being simply the most foolish, yes, and the most heartless nonsense that anybody ever heard of in their entire life, and as being completely out of the question, why, then my shocked denunciator agreed to this notion because of her not ever failing common sense.

Her surrender, though, was based in due form upon the ground that she was sick of arguing about it and just worn to a frazzle by being fussed with and stormed at all day long by people who swelled up like toad frogs.

"Yet my excessive and continual display of so much bad temper," I protested meekly, "and the way in which I continually bully, or so to speak, boss you, my darling, is caused by the fact that neither one of us is any longer able, as Charles City phrases it, to do what we used to could. And I think we ought to face that fact."

She colored up slightly. But she said only that some people were always trying to be funny. She added with hauteur that she did not think they were at all funny, not even if they did happen to have some little book sense, along with very little politeness, if you wanted an honest opinion.

And through an odd coincidence, Mrs. Catherine M. Smith said almost exactly the same thing, a while later on, in a book called *The Devil's Own Dear Son*.

16

How the Hunted Thrived for a While

So BECAUSE of time's pilfering dilapidations, my wife and Ballard and I had begun now to spend five months or thereabouts of each year in Florida; and for ten tranquil years the Ancient and Faithful City of St. Augustine became virtually our home. For Ballard was with us always, to the large contentment of his mother, and to mine too, for that matter.

Ballard had developed into that which the advertisements of "special schools" call tactfully "the exceptional child." His body had grown quite normally, I mean, although it remained dwarfish; but his mind must stay forever—so said the omniscient grave doctors who had made a specialty, along with some opulence, of such mishaps—the mind of a child.

Yet I found as the years passed that his mind was astute and nimble and remarkably well balanced throughout its entire extent. The trouble was, so nearly as anybody can phrase this matter, that a part of his mind was missing. Of mathematics, here to cite his main lack, Ballard had not ever any notion. And in consequence, of any affair into which mathematics entered, such as money values, he had no notion.

But you would never have guessed this, because of his excellent—his actually "exceptional"—powers of memory; his most handsome and stately and extensive vocabulary; his not ever failing bland courtesy toward you, as well as toward any other person; and, above all, his innate gift for acting.

He soon was quite letter-perfect, for example, when it came to reciting his multiplication tables, any one of which he could rattle off with composure and glibness (just as he did a fable or two in the French of La Fontaine) without ever attaching to what he was saying any particular meaning. And the names and faces of every person whom he met he remembered with an accuracy upon which his mother and I learned to depend humbly.

Nor did his ignorance of money at all hamper Ballard in handling money matters. When it came to buying anything he needed—any small article, that is, for with canniness he left the buying of the larger ones to his elders—he would pay for it, invariably, with a dollar bill. With a sedate carefulness he inspected his change before he put it in his pocket. His lips meanwhile moved slightly. You would have sworn he was counting his change. That was what he intended you to think.

And if the clerk told him that this purchase amounted to more than a dollar, then Ballard would apologize courteously for having misunderstood; and produce yet another dollar bill. His acting upon all such occasions was flawless. . . .

But it is not about Ballard I would be speaking except only as the joy which he was to his mother. Her other surviving children she could not retain with her now they were each married, with children of their own to see to; but small, faithful Ballard was hers forever, to be mothered forever, even now that he was approaching his thirtieth year. She would have deplored, and with candor did she grant as much, any miracle which might have made him utterly and how far less lovably normal.

She enjoyed having someone to watch over and to protect, and in brief, "to look after." She delighted always in a combined exercise of affection and of authority. In fact, during the contented while when annually the three of us figured as "winter residents" of St. Augustine, I suspected more than once that this was a pleasure not wholly unselfcomplacent which she got out of most of her dealings with me likewise.

But not out of all of them, I report, with it may be a tint of braggadocio, because I now and then acted exactly like a mule, so I have heard, when anybody was just pointing out what was entirely for my own good; and was getting no more thanks for it than if she were a dog or something. I, in fine, upon these regrettable occasions was enough to drive anybody clean crazy.

In another place, and at sufficient length, I have written as to the life of a winter resident in St. Augustine. My wife enjoyed that placid, if inconsequent, and so neighborly manner of living. It was a wonder to me to note how very quickly she—and Ballard also, because he had inherited his mother's talent, by me uncomprehended, of making friends everywhere—how the two of them, I repeat, appeared to know, and to know quite intimately, everybody in St. Augustine.

Meanwhile she saw to it that every morning I still wrote books undisturbed, in our sitting room upon the ground floor of the Annex to the Buckingham Hotel. Except only for their standing next door to an Air Conditioned Funeral Home, these apartments suited us to perfection; and I had soon learned to accept a few daily obsequies outside my windows as an affair of course which did not at all interfere with one's writing. It followed that year after year we returned to our rooms in the Annex.

My wife and Ballard and I were now not ever separated, not even overnight, throughout the course of ten years. Now that she was crippled, she of necessity had given up attending those patriotic gatherings in Washington—and in Richmond also, now that we were not ever in Richmond during the winter time—those luncheons and banquets and lectures and committee meetings and so on from which she had once got so much hurtless if, to me, unaccountable pleasure. She was not any longer able, simply for my own good, to go with me to New York. In consequence I now stopped going to New York at all; and I thus vanished permanently from the glittering circles of aesthetic intelligentsia. I ceased, in short, to be any longer an ideational gonfalon.

For, what with my wife's arthritis and my persistence in having pneumonia, my wife and Ballard and I now fell into an annual and unvaried routine of living. Throughout the winter we stayed established upon the ground floor of the Buckingham Annex, midway between the hotel itself and the Craig Funeral Home. In April we returned to Richmond, for a month or it might be for six weeks, in which to prepare for our spring and summer stay at Poynton Lodge. And then again, in September, we would go back to Richmond just long enough to make ready for our winter's stay in the Buckingham Annex.

This routine came to content her well enough, I like to remember. She was in pain always; she had learned to accept this fact; moreover, her aspirin tablets, when you took one of them every four hours, did somewhat deaden her pain; and in any case, the unconquerable woman refused to become an old good-for-nothing. She did not intend upon any terms to emulate Grandmother Waddill, and just to sit in a chair.

Priscilla Bradley Cabell, instead, sat in the driver's seat of our car for the most part, driving daily about the Northern Neck of Virginia during the spring and summer, so as to get our household supplies at Kilmarnock, to buy our fish at Sunny Bank, to fetch the day's mail from the post office at Ophelia, or to buy butter and eggs at Gonyon; and besides all these utilitarian outings, to visit informally this or the other farm house of Northumberland where, as everywhere else, she had made friends with whom she delighted to talk, about nothing in particular it might be, but with zest.

Moreover, as I have said, at Poynton Lodge we had staying with us almost always some of her children and her grandchildren, whose affairs needed her supervision simply for their own good. And of these affairs she disposed at once, with a benevolent and cordial competence. She enjoyed doing that.

Then from November until April, in St. Augustine, she enjoyed an unending succession of sedate cocktail parties and of luncheon parties and of card parties and of tea parties. She enjoyed driving down to Marineland for smorgasbord, as they termed luncheon at the Dolphin Restaurant, and she enjoyed driving over to eat shrimp either at Capo's Jungle Inn upon Anastasia Island or at the Bay Gull place upon Corbett's Wharf. She enjoyed driving the eighty miles to and from Jacksonville, so as to do a little shopping, or it might be to attend a Colonial Dames' meeting. She enjoyed driving up town in St. Augustine to the Country Club, or perhaps to the Little Theatre plays in Davenport Park, and driving across town to the plays at the Artillery Lane Playhouse; and she likewise enjoyed driving down town to the exhibits of the St. Augustine Art Association, at which you met and talked with, why, but simply everybody in St. Augustine.

She had, in brief, a talent for living, a talent for

friendliness; and among the no longer youthful winter residents who every year returned to St. Augustine, just as we did nowadays, my not ever resting wife exercised both of these talents to the full.

17

Harps on the Reticence of Marriage

UNDER the unceasing pains of arthritis she had aged, she had aged with a dreadful quickness, in appearance. Her blood pressure, too, inclined nowadays to reach a higher figure than her endless succession of doctors could view with approval. That Mrs. Cabell ought to rest more frequently was their opinion in general; and with about equal profit might they have tendered this bit of advice to Niagara Falls.

But that sounds misleading. That sounds tumultuous. And she was never that. This all-competent woman, I can but repeat, was not ever in any special haste about anything. It was merely that she found hourly something which she but simply had to attend to in person, in a now infirm person.

It troubled me to be seeing the hunched look of her shoulders now that the free and proud poise of her head, which was the first feature I had noted when the two of us first talked together at sunset, was gone forever. It troubled me to be seeing the gray streaks which of a sudden had replaced the gold in her brown hair; and the difficulty with which her stiffened fingers now adjusted a necklace about her throat, or would labor to fasten her earrings. Almost always either Ballard or I had to help her finish getting dressed. And it troubled me beyond reason when that wedding ring, with which I had married her, had to be filed away from her swollen finger, and put aside for all time.

Because, as I pointed out with a painstaking and labored frivolity, for us two to be living together always, alike upon our days out and our nights in, without this traditional badge of matrimony, did not appear quite respectable.

And to this she replied darkly,—

"A great many things are much worse."

That was one of the customary Delphic utterances with which she kept me in my subdued right place. And I had used this phrase, of course; I ascribed it to Dame Niafer, in *Figures of Earth;* but like Niafer's husband, Dom Manuel the Redeemer, I never did find out just what this perturbing reply might mean. Its effect, though, was always to make me conscious of having been up to some rather recent wrongdoing about which I had forgotten, but of which Priscilla Bradley Cabell was remembering every most repulsive and most tiny detail.

Yet howsoever pitiably her body had aged, still her will power and her unconquerable energy and her in-

stinctive friendliness toward all living persons stayed
unshaken. She kept always, and even when every part
of her body was in pain, that habit of smiling suddenly
and brightly just before she began to speak. Her eyes
retained their calm and all-cordial kindliness for whom-
ever she spoke with. The sole difference was that when
her pain-racked, over-driven body was very tired physi-
cally, then the iris of each of her brown eyes would become vividly yellow. I could never understand how this
was possible, but time and again I saw it happen.

There were a great many things about Priscilla Bradley Cabell which I could not ever understand, not even
after some thirty-odd years of marriage. . . .

And I mean—as I wrote at this period, when Nemat-
tanon spoke with his own wife, in *The First Gentleman
of America*—"I mean that actual marriage which has
so little to do with coition. I mean that unbreakable
union because of which we two shall not ever have to
face life lonelily, not ever any more, my dearest, so
long as we both may live. . . . We two need not admire
or love, we may even somewhat dislike, each other.
Yet our alliance is eternal. It endures against all the
world, against every possible happening, and against
evil as well as against good, with the same firmness. . . .
But I cannot tell you what I am trying to tell you. I
cannot say what knowledge it is which moves in my
mind, and which derides me, now that I try to talk
as to our marriage, our true marriage. . . . I mean that
my home is wherever you may be. I mean that I have
faith in you, and in your very gallant, so stupid care for

me, and in your absurd, your idiotic staunchness, now that not any other sort of assuredness remains anywhere."

It was a passage, I remember, which Ellen Glasgow picked out for particular comment.

"—Only you ought to be saying all these so perfectly true things to Percie with your own voice," she told me. "I mean your natural voice, James, the one you so rarely use. And I know you never do say them."

"A considerate and time-tried husband," I returned, "does not overindulge in candor. And in fact, Ellen, whenever I have any special need to hide anything from my wife, then I always print it at full length in one of my books. If ever she came to know the adoring and amused and half-frightened, yes, and the half-fretful way in which I think about her, and about my complete dependence upon her looking after me, she might take advantage of it."

"She knows well enough," said Ellen, and rather gravely. "She does not take any more advantage of it than is good for you. But she would like for you to tell her about it just the same, in your natural voice."

And I am afraid, nowadays, Ellen Glasgow was right.

Still, Ellen had never married. For me to have been telling my wife about how limitless and how all important I found our union, after thirty-odd years of prosaic marriage, would have sounded to both of us absurd, and it would have embarrassed both of us, I believe. So we did not ever talk about any such sentimental matters as what were our emotions toward each other, not any more than—nowadays—we talked about what had been her emotions toward Mr. Emmett A. Shepherd, that downright and practical lumber merchant whom she had loved first and with an admiration which I never inspired in her, nor for that matter, merited.

We accepted, instead, so do I prefer to think, the completeness and the satisfyingness of our mutual devotion tacitly and as an affair of course. We were not so silly as to speak to each other any romantic nonsense about it. Yet I sometimes wish we had shown less common sense.

18

Most of Which Is Quite Commonplace

She had been put to bed by Dr. White, or at least she had not left our rooms in the Buckingham Annex, for perhaps a week, upon account of yet another session with high blood pressure.

Her friends, though, had come so constantly to talk with Priscilla, as she was termed generally by the winter residents of St. Augustine, and they had fetched in such an infinity of candies and of fruits and of bed sacques and of small pillows trimmed with lace, and they had kept her bedroom so vivid everywhere with their flowers—"just like a big funeral" was her smiling yet partly vexed criticism—that the week had passed pleasantly enough, even until her blood pressure had gone down to a satisfactory 165 or thereabouts, and Dr. White had pronounced her arthritis likewise to be more or less under control—"for the present."

The next day she was up and about, immediately after lunch. She did not drive the car that afternoon, upon account of the doctor's general advice "just to take things easy for a while." So it was Helen Gibson who drove for us, across the Bridge of Lions, and then down Anastasia Island, to Crescent Beach, where we paused to chat with Marjorie Rawlings about how splendid it was that Priscilla was up and feeling all right again.

After that, we returned to St. Augustine. We went to the Marks Service Station, so as to get the new car license put on for 1949. Mr. Red Marks, a friend of several years' standing, was pleased effusively to see Mrs. Cabell around once more after her little setback. Then Helen Gibson drove us downtown again, to the Buckingham; and by-and-by, while Ballard's radio was telling us about what had happened in the city of St. Augustine upon 25 March 1949, we prepared for dinner.

Priscilla Bradley Cabell put on, for the first time, one of the two spring dresses which she had bought, and had them altered a little, just so as to have something for the summer. She selected the wine-colored one; and it did quite well for the money. She decided, however, after a prolonged and sidelong consultation with the wardrobe mirror, to stop by tomorrow, now that she was all right again, and to tell Mrs. Bilger to have the skirt let down about an inch more in the back. Because that was the main trouble with the Buckingham. Their food was entirely too starchy.

She was not feeling real hungry. She put aside her

mutton untasted. She, in fact, ate nothing whatever after we had reached the dining room. But she found it certainly was nice, and a change at any rate, to be back over in the hotel. And she was congratulated by everybody—including all the waitresses, I remember— upon her recovery.

A little after eight o'clock, my wife and our son and I walked over to our rooms in the Annex, because Ballard and I were going to the Artillery Lane Playhouse at half-past eight to see *Goodby Once More*. She would not be lonely, though, because Mrs. Duryea wanted to come over and talk to her about something or other, after she got back again into, so it was phrased, that damned bed; and later she would look over the *New Yorker* and the *St. Augustine Record*.

So Priscilla Bradley Cabell began to unfasten the zipper of her brand-new wine-colored dress, and I was brushing my time-thinned hair, preparatory to seeing *Goodby Once More*, when she told me:—

"But I am sick. I must have the doctor."

"Hearing," I replied, "is obedience."

But I was very much frightened now that I had looked at her.

She instructed me composedly, just as she always did in all practical matters, not to waste any time in trying to get Dr. White, because he had told her he, too, was going to the Artillery Lane Playhouse that night. So he would not be at his house now. I might, though, she added, get Dr. Miller.

And with the aid of our telephone I did get Dr. Miller within a quarter of an hour or thereabouts, while Ballard helped his mother to finish undressing and tucked her into bed.

Well, and when Dr. Miller had finished his examination, he said cheerily that, upon the whole, he thought Mrs. Cabell had best go at once to the hospital, where she could have better and more constant service than here in a hotel, while she was getting over this little flare-up.

He was not at all cheery when he spoke with me privately in the hallway. He said simply,—

"It is heart failure."

Then my wife resisted, with a plaintive strange voice, but with indignation also, the notion of her going to any hospital, because Ballard and I would not ever be able to get along without her.

Which, as a general axiom, I admitted, was true; but just for a day or so we could manage perfectly well here at the Buckingham, where everybody knew us.

I tried to speak lightly. But at heart I was sick with terror, because I saw that for the first time since I had known her, my wife was frightened. She knew, I think, what was going to happen. She was wholly sincere, I believe, in saying that the main thought which troubled her was that Ballard and I would not ever be able to get along without her.

So we carried her to the Flagler Hospital. I remem-

ber how limp and helpless her body seemed, in its pink
nightgown, when the two men, who came from somewhere unaccountably, were lifting her body to the tan-
colored canvas stretcher. I remember how I sat beside
her in the dark ambulance, holding both her hands and
assuring her that everything would be perfectly all right
in a day or so, while she kept on repeating that I must
take good care of Ballard, because Ballard had always
been so sweet to her. She was not fully conscious when
we reached the hospital and got her into one of its
rooms upstairs, at the back.

I left her there, drugged and with a professionally
placid registered nurse beside her, toward three o'clock
in the morning. Then I walked alone, all the long way
between Flagler Hospital and the Buckingham Hotel
Annex, in complete darkness, not daring to think about
anything.

She was conscious the next morning. She resented
our not having packed up with her things a hairbrush.

So I promised to fetch it. I deplored, though, her
incorrigible vanity.

"And yet too," I said, as flippantly as I could manage,
to the attendant day nurse, "there was once some little
excuse for it. You may not believe it nowadays, just to
look at her. But when I married her she was a rather
remarkably handsome young woman."

Well, and at that, my wife reached up and she tapped
me upon the cheek. I saw once more, and I saw with

blurred eyes, that sudden bright smile which I had noticed when I first talked with her at the Rockbridge Alum Springs.

"You kiss my foot!" she said, reprovingly, but rather fondly.

She drowsed off after that. And so these were the last words which she spoke to me, or to anyone else.

It was not a romantic utterance. It did not rise to the dignity which is thought to befit a deathbed. Yet I am wholly glad to remember—now—that when she and I last talked together we were both smiling. It pleases me that her very last words, spoken thus gaily, and not without some tinge of affection, as I like to remember too, were a colloquialism of Charles City from which, in vain, throughout thirty-five years, I had tried to wean her away, like an old fuss-budget. No matter what happened, Priscilla Bradley Cabell in this fashion conveyed to me, she did not intend to be bossed by any man alive.

She passed then into a restless stupor which lasted throughout four days. She was in agony, an agony which did not ever desist. Her eyes remained closed. Her mouth moved continuously. Her body also moved continuously, tossing and writhing feebly.

It is not pleasant to remember those four days. Yet I cannot hope ever to forget them, not ever so long as my own life may last.

I knew that her nurses and her doctors were doing all which was possible. But I knew also that I could not make her understand anything. I could not make her understand that I loved her and how much she meant to me. I felt that perhaps I had not ever made her understand about either of these two matters, in a forever vanished time when she had been able to hear me and to look at me with bright and always kindly, maternal eyes.

19

Sundry Reflections Toward Twilight

Yet by-and-by that tortured, forever twisting body, which was all that remained of my wife, was still. By-and-by I was looking at the body of Priscilla Bradley Cabell encased in a pale and silver-trimmed, a white-lined and rigid, and altogether, I reflected, a rather too dapper seeming coffin.

I was alone with her put-by body, now that it had been dealt with properly, by strangers and with chemicals, in the air-conditioned funeral home just next to those rooms in the Buckingham Annex which we had shared, now for ten winters, at a time when she was yet living and had protected always my chosen manner of living. I remembered that.

The mortician, I thought, had so arranged matters as to leave her face quite tranquil now, but somewhat smug-looking. The eyelashes, which I could remember when they were thick and had curved so beautifully, showed thin and straggly, I noticed, now that her eyes were closed forever. Nothing could be done about that. She wore, at any rate, the purple which she and I had preferred for her to wear upon any semi-public occasion, such as a funeral, when she was yet living. She must have a necklace, though, because she had always worn a necklace whenever she was going out anywhere. She had gone now—perhaps—to meet God and Mr. Shepherd.

So I fetched one of her necklaces from our rooms next door, and I arranged it about her neck. I touched up her lips with one of her lipsticks which I found upon her bureau. She would have wanted that done, I knew. She would have termed it something which but just simply had to be attended to.

Then I kissed her upon the forehead. I kissed her lips. I had done this upon the morning that our child was born, I remembered. I had never kissed a dead person before. Her dead flesh, I noted, was not cold. It was lukewarm.

And I spoke to her, because I was remembering a number of matters which I have not recorded in this place. I spoke to her, for the last time, saying,—

"My dear, my dear, we have been through so much together!"

But always together, I was thinking, always together and always united in a complete loyalty to each other, a loyalty which was not garrulous, but which, as we both very well knew, in some sort excluded all other persons. And we were no longer together. We would not ever again be together. . . .

Yet I might try—so my confused thoughts told me—I might try to think I believed that somewhere she still existed; that my actions were known to her; and that by-and-by I would have to render to her an accounting for whatever might remain of my life upon earth. Failing that, I might think—and how far more easily—about myself as being her handiwork, and thus in some sense her monument, inasmuch as a long while before this perplexed and so lonely late March afternoon, I had become a product of the thirty-five years and four months of superintendence, not ever unflavored with a protective, benignant tyranny, which she had allotted to me. In either case, I would have a need to be worthy of her, a need which I knew I could not ever fulfill.

It ought to be sufficient (so did I then recall, upon account of my thirty-five years of enforced correct religious training), it ought to be more than sufficient, to think about her as being established, forever and forever now, in that Episcopalian heaven as to the glories of which she had thought one ought to express a befitting and unswerving belief—through punctilious church attendance, and through being friendly with everybody, and through keeping in an immaculate condition the grounds of Emmanuel cemetery—without anybody's ever prying irreligiously, so did I suspect, into any precise details as to that heaven or as to the clearcutness of her belief.

Hereabouts, though, I encountered difficulties. In any such heaven she, at this instant, would be reunited with her first husband, inasmuch as, to the best of my knowledge, Mr. Emmett A. Shepherd, throughout the latter years of his mortal life at any rate, had been a generally esteemed citizen and a most competent lumber merchant. He had been likewise, so did I now remember, with an obscure and ugly spurt of fretfulness, a vestryman and a member of the Virginia State Chamber of Commerce, as well as being a thirty-second degree Mason. She, at the very bottom of her all-loving and dauntless and her now forever stilled heart, she always would have liked for me to be something of that sort, something really solid and practical, instead of just writing books.

So I could not warm to these notions about heaven. I could not joyously look forward to having my wife present me to her first husband and to the three of us settling down together cosily in eternal bliss. I could not imagine what Mr. Emmett A. Shepherd and I would find to talk about.

That the inheritors of this heaven may neither marry nor be given in marriage I stayed informed notably. And so, so I supposed, in this heaven she would not be married to either one of us. Yet Christ, whatsoever may have been his other attributes, I remembered, spoke as a bachelor. I knew, and I considered this fact quite reverently, a vast deal more about marriage than Christ did.

I knew, for one matter, and I knew beyond doubt,

that my wife and I had reshaped each other gradually, so that the Priscilla Bradley Cabell who had died at Flagler Hospital, in Room Number Seventeen, had become a person noteworthily different from the widow of Mr. Emmett A. Shepherd. He would find some slight difficulty, I thought, in recognizing her.

But above all, I knew that she and I had been married inseparably, throughout thirty-five years, in a union always so increasingly made more intense and more a matter of course that each of us had become, so nearly as my confused thinking could express it, a portion of the other's being. In any second life in which we were not married, we would both of us be incomplete. Yet as angelic spirits we could not hope to be, not ever any more, that so regrettably human, trite, ill-matched, always bickering and all-loyal couple who had shared loyally those forever vanished thirty-five years. And as to the possible supernal meeting by-and-by of two quite other persons—of transfigured strangers, each wearing a halo—I could evoke no interest.

In brief, here in the quiet twilight, the so lonesome twilight, of this air-conditioned funeral home, the promises of the Episcopalian faith failed either to aid or to allure me. I recognized that its putative Jehovah was under no least bond to make intelligible to me His management of heaven, or of earth, or of any other part of His universe. And I must remain an Episcopalian because, upon the off-chance of her still existing somewhere, she would prefer that.

Yet in future I would have to attend divine worship

with a difference. For all that which happens, so our rector would continue to assure us at every Sunday morning service, happened through the will of God. And I must elect not to dispute this. She would not like me to dispute it. Nobody that you ever heard of in Charles City had been that wicked and foolish. But forever now I would have need to regard with some little unavoidable distrust the notion of our being controlled always by an overlord who had condemned the most scrupulous and the most loving of His worshippers to live in never-ending pain for the space of twelve years; and who then saw fit to torture her poor body, malignantly and unceasingly, for a while over ninety-six long hideous hours, before He took her away from me—so far as I knew—forever. . . .

It was about such matters I was thinking confusedly now that I replaced the white, thin, somewhat gritty-feeling veil which covered the face of Priscilla Bradley Cabell, in the Craig Funeral Home, upon Granada Street, in St. Augustine. I never saw her face again.

20

Upon and After the First of April

AFTER that, everything became rather vague and unimportant seeming. The correct formalities for a Virginian gentlewoman of fair prominence had to be honored, of course. So the remains were fetched back to Richmond; a death notice was written and inserted in both the *Times-Dispatch* and the *News Leader;* the pallbearers were selected; there was a half-column about her, or rather, as I noted with a suitable pridefulness, there was somewhat more than a half-column, in each of the Richmond papers; and there was likewise a handsome, quite largely attended funeral, upon All Fools Day, in the graveyard which for so many years Mrs. Joseph V. Johnston and Mrs. James Branch Cabell had kept in fit condition for a handsome and largely attended funeral.

Then the letters and the telegrams of condolence and the visiting cards of the people who had called by the house and asked if there was anything they could pos-

sibly do were sorted out into neat piles, in my library
upstairs—which she had arranged for me to write books
in, I reflected, as I uncovered my typewriter—along with
the resolutions of regret from each one of her patriotic
societies. And I typed out—like an old fuss-budget, I
remembered—an orderly list of these sympathizers, including the post office and the street number of each
condoler, and of the corresponding secretary of each
society.

Next, the proper sort of black-bordered, folding acknowledgment cards were ordered; and we bought for
them, just to begin with, three dollars worth of postage
stamps. In due course all these cards were addressed,
mostly by her daughters—who were careful to use black
ink in place of their customary blue-black ink—and
some few of them by me. But then, it was remarked,
as a fortunate coincidence, I always did use that black
carbon ink which there was so much trouble in getting,
anyhow.

And a special note was added to the folders of the
acknowledgment cards despatched to those persons who
had sent flowers. And in these notes we were at particular pains to specify for exactly what sort of flowers, or
of wreaths, or of designs, or of sprays, we were being
thankful, because for us to do that, so did my stepdaughters point out, was simple, ordinary politeness.
So you wrote down just what everybody sent the minute it came, and then later on you could thank them
for it.

Everything, in brief, alike upon and after All Fools

Day, was conducted quite as my dead wife would have preferred it. And people kept coming to see me and grasping my hand and holding on to it while they said what a splendid woman she had been and how very deeply they sympathized.

I tried to be suitably responsive, in the role of a grief-stricken widower. But everything which was happening appeared to be to be rather vague and unimportant. And at times, even in my present-day contentment, I am visited by the notion that it was not only Priscilla Bradley Cabell who died in St. Augustine after those four days of torture. Some part of me also was murdered, I suspect.

I do not know. I know merely that in this place I have attempted to record, and with an unflawed truthfulness, my memories of that kindly and valorous, brown-haired woman.

And I know, too, that I have not so painstakingly honored convention as to misrepresent my dead wife as having been a super-refined and ethereal, Christmascard angel who—in the phrasing of my epigraph to this book—once flew about our flesh-and-blood world habitually in a nightgown, with an Easter lily in her hand. To the contrary, I have dwelled with a glad particularity alike upon her odd turns of speech, just as they had been preserved among the gentry of Charles City from eras far earlier than the century which our present customs contaminate, and upon those traits in her which I found to be naive or droll, or even irrational; and in which I likewise found enjoyment up to the last day of her living; and to which forever now, so long as my own life may continue, my heart must be harking back all-lovingly.

In brief, I may very well seem, like the protagonist of the first story in which she figured, to have been writing about her life and of its ending as a quaint theme such as I found not unworthy to be commemorated in my Complete Works. But she meant more to me than did all the books in the world.

Book Two:

And Other Amenities

"I dislike also his Southern sentimentality, which leaves him soft when he thinks he is most cynical. One cannot help thinking that, in the impression he gives of living and working in a vacuum, he furnishes a depressing illustration of the decay of the South since the Civil War."

For
and in rogation to my collaborator

Most dear of all that live, when by-and-by
Among these pages leniently you look,
Remember it was you no less than I
Gave birth and being to our second book,
And if its matter seem of doubtful worth
Reflect that I who changed our first design
Exceedingly now note, and not in mirth,
The blunders of our book appear all mine.

21

Seems at Random and Is Far from It

THAT an author may well profit through criticism from the very best informed sources is an axiom no less widely accepted in theory than seldom illustrated in practice. Nevertheless do I propose—as let us say magniloquently, Shakespeare might phrase it—for the nonce to honor this axiom. For it was but the other day that the gentlewoman, who in these times so undisguisedly figures as the head of my household, delivered judgment upon a volume entitled *Quiet, Please*.

She was polite enough, within limitations, as to some sparse features of it. Then, after having summed up its demerits, and especially its just plain coarseness in several places, yes, and what she knew exactly a great many people must have thought about it, she averted from rebuke of the book's contents into yet another form of salutary painstaking. She began, I mean, to speak with a commendable and connubial candor as to my sins of omission.

Because it was all very well for me to make fun of things that I used to be fond of and did not care about any longer, like the novels of Sir Walter Scott and of William Harrison Ainsworth and of lots of other people. I had a right to my own opinion and to change it. Here was a circumstance conceded—with, it was apparent, a few mental reservations—by the person who nowadays knows more about me than does any other living creature. (And that is a fact for which I daily praise heaven upon at least two counts. It would be exceedingly inconvenient to have yet anybody else knowing so much more about me than I do.)

But even so, she resumed, I had not said anything whatever, no, not one word, about any books which I still liked—

"Well—" I explained, in an as copious self-defence as the prosecuting attorney had time to listen to.

Because what about all the other things I liked? And there were such lots of them, too. She just wanted to have me tell her why I behaved in that way. I never wrote a really serious word as to the things, or the people either, that I liked or liked to remember. Instead, I kept on fault-finding about pretty much everything there was or ever had been, and trying to figure in print as being cynical and a highly superior person.

"You!" she then added, in a pensive vein of amazement.

"But I do not!" I replied; and I spoke with no jot or atom, or even an iota, less of firmness than of verity.

Yes, and although for me to be insisting upon this so obvious circumstance was, of course, an orgy in the futile. When once a self-respecting married woman has made any statement to her husband, it is my observance, then she forthwith and forever afterward believes in the truth of this statement—and upon fairly well justified grounds, there is need to admit, inasmuch as with her own ears she has heard this statement advanced by a person in whose sound judgment and in whose garnered wisdom she puts faith, a faith not likely to be shaken by any man living.

I imagine this ability to believe that in dealing with her husband she remains invariably correct and veracious to be one of the two traits common to all fairly contented feminine practitioners of marriage. The other hallmark is, that so over modestly does every successful wife appear to esteem her own value and attractiveness, that no wife worth submitting to seems ever to believe the man who married her could have been born with quite good sense. It is a deduction the results of which she does not always disguise in the home circle; and even in public, strive she never so loyally to humbug her friends and acquaintances, the acute observer can detect of it traces.

Nevertheless are there sundry husbands, and I rank among these enthusiasts, who more or less enjoy being married. So first of all, now that I prepare to confute my traducer—and to flustrate, I hope, her better nature—first of all, shall I list being married to her among the things which I have liked and like to remember.

Which necessitates that I should consider somewhat less personally, and rather more as a quite general practice, this humane compromise with human nature which we call marriage.

And at outset I do not presume to contend that marriage is equally a blessing for both sexes, or that each of them needs regard it with the same seriousness. A wife, to the best of my personal and reverent experience, is no joking matter. Whereas there exist reasons beyond arithmetic through which every married woman is forced to discredit, even though it be only in the back of her mind, her husband's any least claim to be taken seriously.

For she has to live with him. She views him untitivated, by day and at night, in the less captivating aspects of his existence and of his necessities as an animal. And perhaps the more intimate functions of even our leading male mammals cannot always endure this microscopic, hourly scrutiny.

Since it may be that to his direct vis-à-vis no Secretary of State nor any Attorney General appears wholly majestic when once he has become engrossed by a husband's authorized nocturnal activities in expressing affection. A justice of the Supreme Court may seem not utterly awesome when hawking up spittle in the while that his eyes water and his howsoever nobly designed nose trickles with the slimy and shining discharges of

the common cold. Through the congestion of home
life, a bishop or a senator or a professional reviewer of
current reading-matter may have been observed during
the ungainly and opprobrious and distortive postures
requisite for shaving. It is a spectacle which no personal reverence can long survive in the mind of its be-
holder. Nay, even a President of the United States
(during the earlier years of his advancement toward
that eminence) may have been found, in ways which
we needn't go into, an undesirable co-tenant of the family bathroom.

Well, and unavoidably, through these and through
yet other physical phenomena, it follows, after a few
months of matrimony, that the wives of these high dig-
nitaries cannot ever manage later on to admire them
quite so wholly without any reserve as decorum and
ignorance have taught you and me to do. Or at least
I fear not.

Nor hereabouts have I inclined to become coarse un-
necessarily, out of a perverse love for the unlovely, in
parading these truisms. Every man inhabits perforce
a beast's body, and its functioning is perforce bestial,
over and yet over again. Here is a fact which being
married to him must illuminate daily and without reticence. Whereas, still to regard matters from his wife's
point of view, that the feminine body may display an
occasional grossness is neither here nor there, inasmuch
as a rational woman knows of this deplorability a good
while before marriage; and being rational, with a com-
mon-sensibleness not ever granted to mere males, she

will decline to think about any such nonsense anyhow.

These at least are my private personal ideas as to the unromanticizable intimacies of marriage, even though I have been told that all these notions are quite absurd and long out of date. A woman, quoth my informant yet furthermore, is not ever disgusted by any just plain ordinary physical sides of life; she learns about them in childhood as a matter of course; so that she is shocked —and hereabouts I was looked at, as I thought, not without severeness—only when she finds a fullgrown man, yes, and one who was supposed to have a good brain, to show no common-sense whatever as to things which well-bred people prefer not to discuss; and the complete foolishness that I talked about the purity of women's minds sounded simply Victorian.

Nevertheless are these notions innate in me, who, after all, was born and reared and drafted into love's primitive warfare during Victoria's era. And for this reason do I believe we ought to acknowledge, and even to stress as unfrivolously as I have done, that disillusion which marriage must bring about always for what our ancestors used to call refined females—if but in order that we husbands may then applaud with a befitting fervor the loving-kindness which misleads these so diligent and over tender-hearted philanthropists into taking charge of us absurd animals.

I, with all proper seriousness, do not at all understand how they stand it. Yet even in my own household have I known two of them in succession to perform this incredible feat through putting up with me as a husband. And I, astonished by the out-and-out miracle, I have noted amazedly and with a frightened gratitude that men are not worthy of such women as have married me.

However! with due reverence and candor I have set forth the history of my first marriage and of its contentedness and of its demolishment through my wife's death. When she was thus taken away from me, of a sudden and without any least mercifulness, then that special world in which I had existed, and in which I had been more or less shielded and catered to, like a backward child, for all of thirty-five years, was shattered. And to go on living among its bitterly familiar fragments, each one of which in this or the other degree was reminiscent of Priscilla Bradley Cabell, had become a dreary endeavor that I faced unwillingly, or to be more precise about the matter, with a stunned numbness.

For marriage, being a human institution, has, as already I have suggested, its drawbacks, and some of these I have indicated. But the most serious of them all, to my finding, is that, with time, marriage may induce a complete union. I mean that, if to the one side, marriage eventually destroys deference or even any actual love between husband and wife, replacing all passionateness with at best an affectionate toleration,

yet to the other side, does marriage by-and-by establish
for satisfyingly married persons an indispensableness in
each other's living.

They may become, that is, not merely one flesh,
though most assuredly not ever one mind and one
spirit, but for all that, a bifold individual of which
either half confronts always the world and the world's
doings, or even heaven's dim ordainments, with an un-
questioning reliance upon the other half's abettance and
loyalty. Or rather, two persons have somehow been
transfused into one being, a being, it is true, with con-
flicting instincts and inclinations, but an undivided
and, as for the while it seems, an indivisible entity. It is
this quite commonplace and daily miracle, I think,
which makes of marriage a sacrament.

Then by-and-by death severs this entity. And the
husband, or it may be the wife (with women seeming
the more readily resilient), lives on alone, alone both
bodily and mentally, and in a sense, maimed. Contentment and love also may be recaptured later on, as I
myself have learned with an awed gratitude; but they
are regained by, as it were, that which we term nowadays an amputee and a paraplegic. I know, for one,
that a not inconsiderable part of me perished when my
first wife died.

Yet have I made out far more than handsomely with
the surviving remnant of my former self, in that this
remnant has attained to complete complacence and
complete affection with another woman. And my true
point is thus but the identical point which, with an

indulgent shrug, was conceded by Quintus Horatius Flaccus, an appreciable number of years ago, about his not seeming to himself any longer that which he had been under the dominance of benevolent Cynara.

And my being quite consciously another person nowadays, enables me in these quiet final years to look back almost aloofly upon that period in my life throughout which I faced absolute misery without knowing any hopefulness. I was then not conscious in fact of any emotion of any sort; but instead for long months I spoke and I moved in a deeply incurious torpor. So today I find it rather odd, and a matter of mild antiquarian interest, to look back upon that season of my complete bankruptcy as to either thought or feeling, a season throughout which I was not even aware, so nearly as I can now remember, of any grief. I seemed to be fully aware of nothing.

For the only time since I was as yet an undergraduate at college, for the first time in more than a half-century, the will to write had departed from me, and I lived rid of that malady which the learned term *cacoëthes scribendi*. I felt wholly objectless except for the one desire—which was a stubborn but an unviolent resolve, with no fervor in it—the desire, I repeat, to obey my stricken wife's plaintive and persistent, her almost petulant injunctions, uttered so very monotonously and weariedly, in a high-pitched voice which was not any longer her voice, throughout our nightmarish last ride together in the unlighted ambulance which conveyed

her, through the dark streets of St. Augustine in Florida, toward death at Flagler Hospital. Over, and yet
over again, did she then plead with me "to take good
care of Ballard." She thought of nothing else.

For Ballard, I needs here repeat, was our only child,
and a boy (but by now in his thirties) of that retarded
type which an odd euphemism describes as "exceptional." And so it was to the future of his perpetual
immatureness that his mother's last thoughts upon earth
were given over wholly.

Well, but that one desire, with the aid of sundry
physicians, it was that which enabled me to go on
living, I suppose. It in any case was very certainly upon
account of Ballard—or to be accurate, it was through
Ballard's intervention—that I first thought about evad-
ing the stunned loneliness of us both, after Ballard
had surprised, and had in fact dumbfoundered me by
naming, without any preliminaries whatsoever, the real
nice lady whom he would like for me to marry as
quickly as might be arranged.

"—Because, father," as he explained, "she will not
ever put up with any foolishness from you, or from anybody else either."

And he spoke too as one having authority; for with
the person—with, as he then termed her, through one
of his customary enlargements of the English lan-
guage, the "so vibracious" person—whereof he spoke
he had been acquainted from his babyhood onward.

22

Approach to Another Fearless Woman

I HAVE a grotesque need to remember it was in this fashion, and upon these special grounds, that Ballard nominated his wished-for stepmother. I have a need to grant that, until he said this, never had I presumed to think of espousing the gentlewoman in question, whom I had known admiringly and amicably and placidly for a while more than thirty years, ever since my first glimpse of her early in 1918, upon the stage at Belvidere Hall, in the part of an adorable and childlike and a misleadingly meek Nora in *Riders to the Sea*—and then throughout the tumultuous bright times when the two of us had been editors of *The Reviewer*.

Yet furthermore it was at this period (in the surprising role of a major prophet, so do I like to observe nowadays) that I formally went upon record, yes, and upon printed record, as having found it mere time-wasting, as far back as in 1921, for me to dispute about anything whatever with the real nice, so vibracious person whose name, at this so considerably later season, Ballard now mentioned.

Well, and my finding remains unaltered. It follows that the inquisitive may discover upon page 205 of a volume called *Let Me Lie* my most often repeated self-quotation, of latter days, in the home circle,—

"But I did not argue with Margaret Freeman, who waited with her chin raised defiantly."

And I have likewise a need to admit that Ballard's expressed desire then sounded out of all reason. For one matter, the girl (because in derision of time's passage it was always with a tinge of Nora that she entered my thoughts) was by somewhat too numerous years my junior. Biologically speaking at least, I was old enough to be her father. And yet other lacks of alluringness upon my part seemed a large deal too visible to the eyes of honesty.

Upon the other hand, it has been observed by ethnologists that in the male of *Homo sapiens* one just now and then discovers a strain, not here to say of selfishness, but of self-consideration. I considered therefore my deficiencies, when regarded as a potential husband, for no long while; and I weighed instead, at leisure and with an ever-increasing gravity, the fact that always, even from the beginning of our acquaintance, my awareness of this Margaret Waller Freeman had been extraordinarily—so nearly as I can phrase the matter—vivid.

I had not ever thought about her amorously, not for one instant. Off and on, I had heard of, well, but let us thus put it, her mutual interest in various persons; and placidly I had considered these men to be lucky. She was both talented and handsome, I had commented with benevolence, from the status of my sedate seniorship, yes, and in all respects a remarkably fine girl whom any man would be proud to have as his wife. (For here too, I seem to have been prophesying.) With a certain one of these youngsters I had hoped actively for her marriage, I had even encouraged him, for his well-being's sake, to attempt to marry her. I had been sorry when she declined him.

So now did every one of these doings become to me bewildering, because I knew, now, that for near thirty years, in my subconsciousness and without the recurrent action's ever having been noted, the circumstance that this not unpersonable, so emphatic feminine creature existed had been viewed by me, continually, with a wholly singular approval. That—after a thorough deal of deliberation—yes, that appears a fair phrasing for the way in which I invariably thought about her, with a sense of unique and alert and cordial pleasure. She had seemed always, and with an engaging belligerent drollness, to be so vibrantly unlike all other women.

Here then was a fact which had stayed unknown to my obtuseness for a somewhat monstrously long while. Here was a fact, nevertheless; and to me, just somehow, it had become the most important of all conceivable facts.

Which sounds a trifle mixed up, I admit. I have recorded merely my private reflections without any guarantee of their coherence or of their rigid logic, and but as a candid instance of how amorousness may enkindle in a person who, according to popular esteem, is a large deal too old for any more such foolishness.

In short when once I had fair-mindedly thought over Ballard's so surprising suggestion—and without any hurry, for some two months or thereabouts—why, then every day the more certain did I become that my son, that really quite exceptional child, had spoken with a superior inspiration.

So I went a-wooing, gray and in my seventies, no whit unardent. I was emboldened even, just for this once, to argue about any number of matters with the not unnaturally surprised gentlewoman involved.

And time proved, time has most handsomely countersigned, the wisdom of my senescent hardihood. Time has found me, so one might express it, subjoined to an unutterably efficient and always improbable, tense and usually indignant about something or other and not ever dubious-minded person (born too, like the first intrepid woman who married me, under candor-speaking Virgo), who nowadays controls my doings, and who pampers me with an abrupt yet tender discretion. Time,

in brief, has provided for me contentment—in a reasonable degree, I append hastily, so as here to avoid that
boastfulness which the gods mislike and are shrewd to
punish, terming it *hubris*—and time has renewed in me
a civil interest as to life in general, now that I find
myself to be communing daily with a blend of Aspasia
and Joan of Arc and Mrs. Nickleby.

Yes, for I beyond doubt am not troubled, as John
Milton, in his *Doctrine and Discipline of Divorce*, declared himself to be annoyed, by "a mute and spiritless
mate"; but instead am I blessed with, and at times
quite volubly, just that same "intimate and speaking
help" of whom Milton then voiced his need.

Much more than certainly I would not have the outcome to be at all otherwise. For as yet (still am I being
very careful about *hubris*), as yet do I rejoice in this
vehement person who once seemed to me so unbefit-
tingly my junior, and who nowadays, although with a
fairly polite reticence about it, is at especial pains to
control me always as being a regrettably shiftless infant.
There can lurk (I hope) no flagrant or Zeus-provoking
braggartism in granting that I have come to regard her
with an intenseness of amused and admiring affection
such as I not infrequently, in view of my advanced stage
in life, consider with wonderment.

"But how clumsily over-imitative of Molière," I observe upon these analytic occasions, "appears the char-
acter of this age-ridden, fond dotard!"

Whereafter I at once, and with my fingers crossed,

remark yet again, and with a well called-for humbleness, that men are not worthy of such women as have married me.

I grant, then, that I have liked, and that I still like to think about, both of my wives.

Hereabouts, though, the thought occurs that to be admitting in print you rather like your wife, and to be rehearsing the causes and defining the nature of this, after all, not blameworthy or infrequent husbandly feeling, is for some unformulated and murky reason adjudged to be, during her lifetime, indelicate.

Should she predecease you, then is your freedom enlarged to make public your affection alike in talk and in the terms of her epitaph, or should you elect for extremes, in a full-length elegy. Some dolorous and honeyed protestation of this sort is, indeed, expected of every widower; so that by a droll enough turn, one may note even John Milton's aforementioned "mute and spiritless mate," when once she was buried, to have become in a fine sonnet his "late espousèd saint." And just that during her earthly existence is precisely what, you are certain, he never called her.

Well, but nevertheless must I presume to defy this convention of taciturnity during your wife's lifetime as to her more amiable qualities, because as I began by explaining, I have been put under a mandate to write here concerning a handful of affairs and a few people whom I have liked or like to remember. And since there is nothing which I like better nowadays than I do the personality of the person who issued this mandate, I could not honestly nor without an horrific twinge of conscience omit a summary of her traits and of her goings-on from any catalogue of my life's amenities. So instead do I prefer intrepidly to violate the canons of Miltonic or at any rate of genteel good taste by admitting, despite her present and her how very omnipresent vitality, that I rather like my wife.

I, in point of fact, am afraid that I have come to like this Margaret Cabell completely and gladly—without, as the phrase runs, any ifs or ands about it, and with a sort of paternal exultant pride in her, and with a judicious abundance of submissiveness, and with zest. And I do not intend dumbly to await the horrible off-chance of first expressing any one of these facts in an epitaph.

For when we look back upon the past, it is my experience, then the dead years are thronged with far too many sad and accusing ghosts of those whom we loved without ever voicing to them articulately the extent and the depth of that love.

"I understand you now," each phantom seems to be saying. "But why did you not tell me just how very much I meant to you when I wore flesh and blood, which would have quickened and would have been made glad by your speaking? Today it is too late, and too late forever. The dead may forgive the living—almost—but they cannot love the living; and the living do well to distrust the dead."

23

About Books and How Writers Happen

Aʙᴏᴠᴇ all, though—here to hark back a few pages—
if the intimacies of marriage needs deny to any fairly
rational woman the privilege of regarding her house-
mate quite seriously, yet above all, must the wife of a
professional writer consider her husband to be ludicrous
entirely, in that his work, as the rule, calls for an assumption on his part of an unhuman fair-mindedness
and, even at times, of his omniscience.

With but one droll exception (upon which I am
planning to comment by-and-by), he needs to pretend
that he speaks without prejudice concerning—and that
he really does know everything about—whatever themes
he may be discussing. Whereas his wife has perceived
long ago that, in point of fact, the impractical and opin-
ionated and muddle-headed creature does not know
very much about anything. It now and then indeed
may be a part of her province to see that he doesn't.

His enforced posturing, however, is an antic which in no way seems to lessen her endurance in putting up with his perpetual presence around the house. A fair percentage of gifted writers, there is no denying, do turn out to be insufferable in the role of a husband—but only, I believe, those untactful typists who have not learned how to attempt a civil disguise of the circumstance that with them the development of their writing comes first, and the preferences of any living woman second. Their wives, I believe also, comprehend this at bottom; but so long as the moonstruck long-legged child stays thoughtful enough to try to hide his idiocy, they very often condone it.

I do not know why they should. I myself would never stomach a rating thus plainly subservient, not for one instant, were I in their shoes, or more aptly to paraphrase the conjunction, in their *robes de nuit*. But I do know that I wonder over the fundamental patience, as distinguished from mere conversational stilettos, of any woman able to endure being the wife of a creative writer who takes his art quite seriously. For only a part of her husband is married to her; and that which he thinks to be the more important portion of him is daily about this or the other supernal affair of the heart among the flawless phantoms and the demi-goddesses evoked by his day-dreaming.

The more important portion, I repeat, in his own private opinion, which may very well be mistaken. At any rate, I most certainly do not go so far as to agree nowadays, or not without several million reservations, with Miramon Lluagor when he declared:

"There is no marriage for the maker of dreams, because he is perpetually creating finer women than earth provides. The touch of flesh cannot content him who has arranged the hair of angels and modeled the breasts of the sphinx. What has the maker of dreams, what has that troubled being who lives inside the creature which a mirror reveals to him, to do with women?"

Well, I can see what the speaker meant. Yet I think that Miramon here deals with just one aspect of the married life of a creative writer and rather unconscionably exaggerates this particular aspect. For I know with a befitting gratitude that at least two women, each one of whom became my wife, have been dear to me beyond words, and each one of them very far more dear than are all the books in the world.

But to go back to the point which the present-day custodian of my personal welfare has raised, I am afraid that no book can retain forever its magic unimpaired for any one reader, no matter how admirable he, in theory, may still find this book to remain. A book, be it never so magnificent and adroit, has just so much to offer, and no more, in the way of enjoyment, or rather, in the way of a diversion from its reader's set round of living. When once you have savored to the full that diversion, your indulgence in which may survive a number of re-readings, then by-and-by the book of necessity palls. It becomes to you pervasively stale because all of it is familiar. Your frame of mind, in brief, is not unlike that of the person who found *The Tragedy of Hamlet, Prince of Denmark,* to be rather too full of quotations.

I pause here to meditate a trifle forlornly upon the writers a fair quota of whose work my judgment still admires. I recall, at almost complete random, Lucian and Horace, Villon and Montaigne and Marlowe, Sir Thomas Browne and Molière, Wycherley and Congreve and Sheridan—along with Thackeray and Dickens and Robert Browning and the elder Dumas, of course—as well as Stevenson and Kipling, and not at all forgetting Arthur Machen and Walter Pater, or even (within more narrow limits) Oscar Wilde and Saki. And dozens upon scores of yet other geniuses. "A fair quota," I repeat, because in the Collected Works of each of them, as of every other known author, there is overmuch which I would far more than gladly see obliterated.

In all these writers I have rejoiced. Concerning many of them I have emitted pæans. Well, and I still like them, yet it is with a difference. In each of them I can still find that element which once upon a time ensorcelled me, and of that element my judgment today approves. But the approving is no longer fiery; it has dimmed as to enthusiasm; it is judicial merely; and in consequence it lacks gusto.

I admire, in fine, an all-familiar excellence which, to me, has become an affair of course. Others it may rouse to well merited loud plaudits delivered upon wholly logical grounds, but not me, not ever any more, no more than may the caretakers of the Louvre pause daily to marvel at the Venus of Milo. Or rather, in every instance the conceded skill or the undenied genius of the writer has become as the charms of a woman whom one has loved ardently, and whom one has possessed completely, for no single evening but over and yet over again. The beauty and the dearness of her may stay unaltered; you may well have become more deep-heartedly fond of her: but the rapture of which you were conscious at first, when the details of her body and her ways of satiating you with ardor and contentment and languor were a novelty, is not ever to be recaptured. Here is perhaps an indelicate analogue begotten by lubricity; but I take it to be exact enough.

So then does it become one of the minor penalties in the elderness of a devotee to literature that he reads in any and all noble books with a diminished zest. "Reads in," do you let me repeat, because I find that, while constantly I revert to many books which my youth, or to be more exact, my relative youth, admired, it would never occur to me, not nowadays, to invade any one of them formally and foreplanning a journey from the first chapter to the last. Instead, I peruse benignly and snugly, amid familiar surroundings, this or the other favored passage, whether it be of description or of narrative or of dialogue, dawdling among time-tested friends; and our re-encounters are wholly pleas-

ant, in a sedate fashion, but without any earth-stagger-
ing excitement.

As go the fire-new books of today, and even the
very latest masterworks of their publishers' more widely
advertised adulation, they tend, almost all of them, to
leave me unfired with enthusiasm.

For one matter, my Scots blood, without exactly boil-
ing over, does at least appraise with a heightened tem-
perature the price of books nowadays. But yesterday,
or to be wholly accurate, but yesteryear, so does thrift
reflect, a full-length new novel—applaudably bound
and well printed—was purchasable, if you went to the
right places, at $1.07. Here is a fact which now seems
as fantastic as a bit of Ceylonese folklore or as the
promises of a campaigning politician or as a Little Lord
Fauntleroy suit.

But above all am I prone, in assaying our current
novelists, to feel that their aims and their touchstones
appear not mine. Almost always the author's assumptions as to the nature and the thoughts and the resultant doings of men and women, and his manner of
transcribing his various aberrations—for so needs I consider them—seem to me alien. I reflect that human
beings (whom, after all, I have seen and known and
been diverted by for some seventy-odd years) are simply
not as he depicts them.

And I have no special quarrel with what I take to
be this parade of the writer's obtuseness. It does not in-

terest me, that is all. I grant freely that he (or perhaps she) may be right, and I wrong; *Homo sapiens* may have changed utterly since I last observed, or endeavored to portray, this subdivision of fauna; yet at bottom I dare to disbelieve in any transformation so thorough; and there is no denying I incline to lay aside what appears to me the youngster's bungling but languidly and incompletely read.

Yet this verdict, doubtless, is the verdict of hardening arteries and abating animal heat and still other deteriorations. I do not gravely question that today the cause of literature may be flourishing, with never so many everliving masterpieces as plentiful among these —to me—uncongenial volumes as are blackberries in August. It very well may be that to my juniors' merits time has blinded me, so do I elect to grant humbly and with unconcern. Because it is certain that, just somehow, their standards seem not to be my standards, nor do their goals appear the ends toward which I have striven. My standards and my aims, like those of the Chaldeans or of the Edomites, have no doubt become outmoded, that is my final verdict after inspecting most of our recent novels.

For therein (to my so frankly fallible judgment) seem not to prosper the auctorial virtues to which very long ago I pledged my allegiance. I mean, of course— as upon occasions beyond calculating I have repeated— the virtues of distinction and clarity, of beauty and symmetry, of tenderness and truth and urbanity. These qualities my obtuseness does not find blended, not to

any sufficing degree, in the more widely admired novels
or treatises or other literary masterworks of today; my
insensibility perceives no attempt to blend these qualities; and in consequence I cannot care gravely, either
with applause or frowns, about books which seem to
ignore the particular virtues that, now for a half-century, I have preached and pursued and fallen how far
short of! I leave such books unread, or else, I read them
but fractionally.

But not fractiously. My indifference hereabouts does
not ever, do you let me protest, imply any out-and-out
dislike. It is merely an evincement of the firm faith
of a zealot in the especial creed, the revered formulae, to
which his lifetime has been devoted. Those who do not
accept this creed he, as an affair of course, believes to be
aesthetically damned; yet he does not with any deepness fret over this circumstance, not any more than (I
imagine) does an efficient rector, or even an arch-
bishop, habitually lie awake at night bewailing the
billions of Hottentots and of Buddhists and of Moslems
and of limitless other heretics who, his convictions assure him, are either en route for, or else are already
populating, hell's taller flames.

"A creed," I have said, "to which his lifetime has
been devoted." And I begin to wonder just how any
such creed is come by? Or in other words, how does a
writer who takes his art at all seriously happen now
and then to occur?

Concerning only one of these fanatics is my information more or less thorough; and I question if heredity or any other impulse recognized by the pathologist could have played any part in my vague but firm resolve, from my childhood onward, "to become a writer." I know that my surroundings contributed to this resolve nothing.

I am not denying that at a season more or less earlier than my childhood the senior members of my immediate family had perused, in addition to the multitudinary *Readers* of William Holmes McGuffey and yet other schoolbooks, a novel or so by Sir Walter Scott, or by Bulwer-Lytton, or by John Esten Cooke. And in those days, of course every well-thought-of Virginian household had its library sitting room, with at least two bookcases entombing behind glass, just as all other coffins customarily did then their occupants, a staid and serried cohort of English classics in courtly bindings untarnished by usage. But the well-bred Richmonder, by and large, after the manner of my father and my uncles, confined his reading to the local papers, finding that the *Dispatch* in the morning and the *State* in the evening contented all literary needs.

As for the gentlewomen, what with the housekeeping and their church and their social duties, and then the children too of course, why, but there you were! Books might be all very well in their place, but where was the time to read them in? Thus quoth my aunts and my mother also, in a dismissive unanimity.

My grandfather, I admit—because I had only one

grandfather, Dr. Robert Gamble Cabell, with my Grandmother Cabell up in the higher circles of his Second Presbyterian Church heaven long before I was born—had read most of the tales of Edgar Allan Poe; but merely so as to find out whatever people saw in them, because that writer and he had been schoolmates; and while he declared some of them to be pretty good stories, still the fact remained that he had not ever thought much of Edgar except as a right fine swimmer.

So my only grandmother, Mrs. James Read Branch, alone among my vast family connection read books with any frequentness; and besides that, she was in some yet other ways, I thought, an unusual person whom I liked and still like to remember.

Which would seem to make it a part of my assigned duty herewith to tell you about my grandmother.

24

As to Childish Matters of Long Ago

My GRANDMOTHER was born a Patteson—Martha
Louise Patteson—to begin with (nor was there any
crime more outrageous, such as a mere rape or a murder, than to spell "Patteson" with an *r*); and her husband, who was drowned some ten years before I under-
took the hazards of human living, had been likewise
her second cousin. She had loved this, as I thought
from his portraits, rather dictatorial- and peevish-looking
James Read Branch with a complete devotion which
survived him throughout the thirty-nine years of her
widowhood up to her last moment on earth. "Colonel
Branch," to her finding, had been flawless. But at that,
Grandmother did not ever weigh the fantastic notion
of the Branches' being the social peers of the Pattesons.
This point was not stressed. It was but a tacit axiom
tactfully not dwelt on.

142

In any event, she did marry "Cousin Jimmy," as throughout the first twenty-five years of her living she had called this, to my immature judgment, somewhat grim-looking person who scowled at you from between side whiskers, sort of as if he didn't much like your being named after him. But once my grandmother and he were married, then she of course, at the commands of Virginian etiquette, referred to and addressed him always as "Mr. Branch." When The War came on— and as I have recorded elsewhere, in the Virginia of my youth, so far as my elders were concerned, there had never been in the world's history but one real war, this being the carnage which "Mr. Lincoln" (as he was termed aloofly) had started in 1861—why, but then before long my grandmother's husband had become to her, conversationally, "Colonel Branch." And Colonel Branch he remained forever afterward.

He was wholly perfect. There was never a better or more loving and attentive husband. I was told, it is true—but I was told casually, during a condescending philippic of which the target was a quite other person —about that wartime incident when Grandmother, coming unexpectedly into the room, had found the wife of his commanding general in the Army of Northern Virginia sitting in Colonel Branch's lap and slobbering all over him with her big, wet, spitty kisses. Which simply showed you just what sort of a person that nobody from Charles City, or somewhere else down there, really was. And so Grandmother had told the woman at once, right to her face.

"But, Grandmother, weren't you mad with Grandpa too?"

"Why, but of course I was not angry with Colonel Branch," she replied, a trifle surprised. "Men never do have any sense about things like that, and nobody expects them to."

Which statement I, upon reflection, find to embody a fairly substantial section of our former Southern mores.

Well, then, but after The War, Colonel Branch went back into the Produce Commission business; and within four years he had put by what in those days was considered an ample fortune. And so when he was drowned in the July of 1869, along with a policeman, through their being pinned down in the James River under a collapsing bridge, then Grandmother became the richest widow in Virginia, or as it was reputed, in the entire South, still in her thirties.

She was handsome, too, with the dark and clear-cut, somewhat Spanish features of all the Pattesons. So before long there were any number of gentlemen who endeavored to become Colonel Branch's successor.

She refused each of them civilly, because as befitted a Patteson, she was always courteous to and concerning everyone (excepting, it is true, that nobody from down in Charles City, whose prominence at so many Confederate reunions my grandmother resented continually with a partly amused scorn), but I am afraid all these polite rejections had a tinge of hauteur. She did not think that a real gentleman would ever marry a widow, she explained to me. You could not respect any man who would take another man's leavings.

It is pleasing (and yet wistfully depressing also) to remember the days of her affluence when Grandmother owned the big house at First and Franklin Streets, where the Richmond Public Library now stands. Her rambling three-storied mansion and its grounds then occupied about half of the block, with a hedged flower garden, having also a few smallish fruit trees in it, to the front and the east; and with an enormous catalpa tree —surrounded by a circular wooden bench, I remember—and a substantial stable in the rear, as well as a smoke house and a sort of storage hall with several rooms up over top of it for the servants to live in. There were two horses and two cows and a small vegetable garden and some large grape trellises all back there too, in Grandmother's so very big back yard.

So that the place was really a minor plantation in what is nowadays a business section of downtown Richmond. And my ability to remember these matters I have found to be wistfully depressing, do you let me explain, in that it causes me to feel not at all unlike a survivor of some Pliocene or Cro-Magnon tribe and its social orderings.

Anyhow, there Grandmother lived in state in a tiny Richmond where everybody knew everybody else, and

where most of the population seemed to be Grandmother's cousins. You wondered how on earth she kept
track of all those cousins.

On week days every morning Grandmother would
ride down town, in her big carriage with her two horses
pulling it, to the Sixth Street Market and buy everything she needed. Then Jackson, that fat and sort of
solemn-looking colored man who was her coachman,
and in a real fine uniform with nice shiny buttons to
it, would drive the meat and the vegetables and the
eggs, and whatever else there was, back to the house
in the carriage while Grandmother walked home. She
did not have to walk but seven blocks, yet it most always took her right much time to walk them, because
she would have to stop on the street and talk to such
lots of her friends, or maybe she would go into this or
the other cousin's house just for a little visit, or perhaps
to look at the new baby. In those days nearly every one
of the married ladies had a new baby every two years.
And in those days nobody was ever in any special hurry
about anything, anyhow. So Grandmother would very
often not get home until almost two o'clock and barely
in time for her dinner.

But on Saturday afternoons she would send you
down to Mr. Ferrandini's, over on Broad Street, right
underneath your dancing school, to ask for "that pack-
age for Mrs. Branch," and you would bring it back for
her. It was a wrapped-up small flat box, real light to
carry, and you were not supposed to know what was

in it. But you did. It was Grandmother's front hair.

Ladies did not wear any false hair, of course. False hair was just plain tacky. But lots of ladies put away their combings in a little round box on the bureau until they had got enough saved for Mr. Ferrandini to fix up into a front or into a switch, or sometimes into little separate curls which you stuck in with a hair pin wherever you wanted to. And each one of these was made out of the ladies' own hair entirely, so that it wasn't false hair. And Grandmother used to have her front all stiffened up or frizzed or washed, or something, every Saturday, so that she could wear it to St. Paul's Church on Sunday morning and look extra nice while she listened to Dr. Minnigerode preach.

For Grandmother was "on the board," whatever that meant, of the St. Paul's Church Old Ladies Home, over on Leigh Street, and she was on the board of the Ladies Hollywood Memorial Association, and she was always being put on boards to get up bazaars to help something or other that was Confederate. So she kept pretty busy. And besides that, she gave heaps of parties, and she had what people called tableaus and sometimes whole plays in her back parlor which you were allowed to sit up to.

You went to her bazaars too, over at the Richmond Blues' Armory, where Grandmother bought for you, from the gentleman who made up all sorts of shiny glass things right while you were looking at him, a ship wtih sails and everything in a foamy little round ocean.

But for your brother Robert she got two bright colored birds with long necks drinking out of a pink fountain, with the fountain part of it shaped sort of like one of those champagne glasses that Grandmother used on birthdays in the family.

Those bazaar things were made of what people said was spun glass. And that was a funny name for it, you thought, because the real foreign-looking gentleman at the bazaar did not seem to be spinning anything, but instead he blew his glass into the shapes he wanted with a little tube. Anyhow, they were made out of his sort of glass, the ship and the birds and the ocean and everything, and each of the two presents was under a kind of rounded-off shaped, right tall cover made out of just plain glass. The covers were pretty much like the cover that your Grandfather Cabell and heaps of other people had over the parlor clock, and the covers kept the ship and the birds from getting broken or having dust on them.

Both of those spun-glass ornament things stood on the mantelpiece in the nursery at your house for a long time. They were so shiny and so mighty cheerful looking they were just beautiful, you thought; and Grandmother was always giving nice presents like that to you and to almost everybody.

When the Confederate Memorial Day came around, then Grandmother would take you and her next biggest grandchild, Thomas McAdams, out to Hollywood Cemetery for two or three days before it was Memorial Day, so that you could help about fixing the flags and the wreaths and the other designs and about keeping the flowers watered upon dead people's graves who were kin to Grandmother, and in Colonel Branch's section especially. She was always right solemn about Confederate Memorial Day and about that Mr. Lincoln.

She had a signed picture of the gentleman who had killed him, along with a pack of cards the gentleman had sent to Colonel Branch. Colonel Branch and Grandmother had known Mr. Booth when he was a play actor in Richmond in what people called a stock company.

Well, and at first Grandmother thought Mr. Booth had done a fine thing when he shot Mr. Lincoln, but later on she decided that maybe it was a mistake, because perhaps if Mr. Lincoln had gone on living he would have been nicer and kinder to the South than those Carpetbaggers were. Mr. Lincoln had meddled with the South when he had no business to, and he was an awful tacky person. Everybody knew about how he had left five dollars for his wife upon her mantelpiece the next morning after they got married. Which simply showed you just what sort of women he was used to. But then almost all Yankees were tacky; and lots of people said Mr. Lincoln had meant well.

You thought privately that five dollars was a mighty nice present, but something told you this was one of the things which grown-up people knew about, and you didn't. So you did not argue about it. And, in fact, very few persons ever did argue with Grandmother.

She was just set in her ways, and that was all there was to it.

It may be inferred that my grandmother was "unreconstructed." She was. Even up to the end of her life the fall of the Confederacy, some forty-three years earlier, remained to this now age-stricken gentlewoman a never forgotten personal loss, a loss as irreparable as had been the death of Colonel Branch. I do not mean that she was ever lachrymose about either; but merely that her devotion to the memory of the Confederacy and of Colonel Branch stayed at all times sacred.

Or as another grandson, my own, if some deal incongruous, revered first cousin, the Reverend Walter Russell Bowie, has written concerning her: —

"To a woman like Martha Branch, devotion to the past was nothing less than religious; to a cool outsider it would have seemed fanatical. Any question against what she regarded as the unsullied record of the South was blasphemy; and any sign of compromise toward the northern enemies was a moral lapse."

All of which I endorse as being, for a minister of the gospel, a remarkably sound and temperate statement.

I have spoken thus far of the days of her affluence alone as my first childhood observed them, howsoever briefly; for by the time I was ten or thereabouts Grandmother had spent cheerily almost the last penny of Colonel Branch's money, just somehow. Nobody ever knew quite how, and least of all did she. The once largest fortune in Virginia lasted her, though, for near twenty magnanimous years, throughout which economy and my grandmother remained total strangers, and profuseness and generosity stayed her hourly companions. To anybody who was in trouble, I mean, but in particular to anyone who was blood kin to her, or to any public cause of which she approved, she immediately and with eagerness gave whatever was needed—or to be wholly accurate, whatsoever was asked for—as befitted a Patteson. To do that was her code. The resultant, the inevitable, poverty and the twenty years of dependence upon her nearer relatives, of whom but yesterday she had been the free-handed patroness, and the disappearance of her bodily health—all which followed—she faced not one whit less cheerily.

So by and by did Grandmother become a little, bent gray wisp of feebleness who never quitted her bedroom nowadays. Yet still she enjoyed life; she existed vicariously but with a lively vigor in every least concernment of her five children and of her eleven grandchildren; so that through her fathomless love for them her interest in life stayed always vivid and benevolent and quietly garrulous even until her life had ended, of a sudden and without pain, upon the eve of her seventy-seventh birthday.

Well, and it was then that forthwith I got the notion of the dear heaven of Jurgen's grandmother, into which the rejuvenated pawnbroker was to climb upon Jacob's Ladder a considerable number of years afterward.

Because I knew exactly how my own grandmother, now that she was dead, would be dealing with the not impossible Proprietor of this universe, whom my story fabled to be called Koshchei, and how He would never be able not to humor her. For this reason then did Martha Louise Patteson Branch, in the guise of Steinvor, enter into the tale triumphant over all reason, whether human or divine; and Koshchei created out of hand, for her inhabitance, that special sort of heaven which she had expected and so well merited.

All which I have told you thus far you may have found to be appreciably remote from the circumstance that, alone among my immediate relatives, my grandmother read books. But in any case, she did. She indeed was that which wholesomely unpedantic persons— such as without qualms "realize" that so and so has happened, and become "intrigued" by this or by the other "phenomenal" occurrence—call an omnivorous reader.

She had finished with most of the standard classics of English and American literature a good while before my time; and Grandmother had dismissed them affably. Never again did she return to these time-honored volumes, during at all events the latter years of her life, but rather did she read, persistently and with zest, the novels of Miss Marie Corelli, and of Charlotte M. Braeme, and of Ouida, and of "The Duchess," and of Mary Elizabeth Braddon, and of Charlotte M. Yonge, and of Mrs. Henry Wood, and of Mrs. Forrester, and of yet many other no longer world-famous gentlewomen who, during those far-off days, specialized in high romance and as a rule (or so at least did I, who was not familar with their masterworks, surmise) in the upper classes of English society.

For my grandmother's demands of literature were both simple and explicit. I know because very often she sent me down to the Rosemary Library to return the three books she had finished with and to bring back three new ones.

"And try to pick out," were my instructions, "at least one love story with a duke in it."

"But why do you want a duke, Grandmother?"

"Well," she replied, and a whit wistfully, "I have known pretty much all sorts of people in my time excepting them. No, I never knew any dukes, and so of course I like to read about them."

This was logic, one felt, with a flaw in it somewhere. Yet I think otherwise today. She was but calling upon art to fulfil art's proper function, of supplementing life. Her own life had been ever busy and happy enough and duly encolored with grief and made holy by ever-abiding love. Her life had satisfied her amply. But after all, there had not been any dukes in her life.

Nor was it that at some unbalanced moment my grandmother had thought a duke (or for that matter, any other creature living) to be the superior of a Patteson. It was merely that this outlandish species of fauna had chanced to interest her through the not tepid reports, or so I gathered, rendered by almost every one of the aforementioned authoresses as to the habitual goings-on of a duke. There was nothing whatever like it in Richmond, and there never had been, not during her lifetime anyhow.

For this reason, then, did my grandmother delight to read about dukes, or in default of their fellowship, about the gilded depravity of their inferiors in the peerage; and she alone of my immediate family ever read any books at all in the fields of creative writing. And so my own trend toward what is termed "escapist" fiction must have been inherited from her, says logic hereabouts, with that smug chuckle-headedness which is customary among littérateurs and our more eminent statesmen.

Yes, but logic thus compels me to consider fiction logically.

25

Expounds on Fictions about Fiction

Now, to start with, I could never understand how this prattle about escapist fiction ever came into vogue among persons who, in at least a fair number of other respects, seem rational. All fiction, I reflect of necessity, is escapist in that it frees the reader from the set round of his daily living and enables him to play at being somebody else. Here is a truism upon which I discoursed never so many years ago in a volume called *Straws and Prayer-Books;* but without stressing sufficiently, I fear, the essentially escapist, not here to say irrational, nature of that element in literature which the incurably naive term "realism."

For this realism also is a quite seriously regarded creed, I take it; and so as to illustrate some tenet of this creed does a realistic novel become a venture into sermonizing. (And the romanticist is equally a sermonmonger, with the difference that he preaches from another creed.) What puzzles me is that among realists

155

the unvarying text of all their sermons should run always, so nearly as I can phrase this heresy,—

"God, but isn't life awful!"

Whereafter of course the realist may develop his theme in countless manners. He may treat it with gravity, with flippancy, or even with a tender sympathy for life's victims. He may become witty about it, or ironic, or blasphemous, or he may wax stolidly hard-boiled in the terse rhetoric of a telegram. Nor are the higher peaks of poetic prose denied to his proud ascent. Still, however, does his assumption remain always,—

"God, but isn't life awful!"

Now the immediate sophism hereabouts is that to the reader, whether snug in his library or, to the detriment of his eyesight, semi-recumbent and all comfortable in bed, life is not awful, not at any rate just then. He to the contrary is enjoying life. And from that enjoyment he is pleased to escape through playing condescendingly at being the protagonist of a realistic bit of fiction. His imagination of its own will descends into sordidness or brutality or self-conscious failure or mere blind bewilderment or, which is perhaps most droll of all when you come to think of it, into crass illiteracy and its attendant drawbacks.

Yes, even in the act of reading, he can play at being a person to whom reading is an unmastered accomplishment! Here is a fact which, I admit, quite thoroughly staggers me through its revealment of the incredible compass of human fancy. And if these various imagina-

tive wanderings among invented degradations and dis-
comforts be not escapism from the reader's actual personality and surroundings, I know not how to label the
paradox.

Yet furthermore I regard this "God, but isn't life
awful!" school of fiction, in any one of its multitudinous
forms, as being a stubborn perversion of veracity. It
reminds me, through a homely turn, of the person to
whom I listen most frequently nowadays, and of her
habitual classing of all fermented beverages as "alcohol." Over and yet over again have I pointed out to the
woman that even the most potent of them are but fifty
per cent alcohol. (Not that my logic has any least effect
upon her.) And I think ugliness and gloom, or any
sense of self failure, or a suspicion of one's personal
inconsequence, to compose, upon the whole, a considerably smaller fraction than fifty per cent of most human
lives.

I think that to the contrary for well-nigh every man,
in his own wholly private and judiciously unvoiced
opinion, life is a romance in which he is the main char-
acter, nay, even the hero. That life should very often
treat him unjustly or cruelly he accepts as being the
customary manner of any other romance in dealing
with its hero. His misfortunes are but temporary im-
pediments in his progress toward the very public defeat
of his persecutors and the attaining of unending opulence and ease and contentment, by-and-by and just
somehow, through happenings which it is not necessary
for him to imagine with definiteness.

Tomorrow, in brief, or at worst the day after tomorrow, is about to prove an all-glorified version of today. It is with this innate belief that every human being is born and by virtue of which he lives. And except for this irrational optimism, I make no doubt, the race would long ago have resorted to mass suicide. But man's stubborn optimism defies reason, it stays unshaken by mere facts, because it is the core of human nature, impregnable so long as human nature exists. Yet realists, so far as ever I have dabbled in their products, would deny to their puppets the unfailing narcotic, the mild inebriation, nay, the pot valiancy of this same optimism which so plainly, to my experience, as a working rule keeps life more or less livable for everybody. One really does wonder at the effrontery of writers who can dare thus high-handedly to misrepresent such an omnipresent phenomenon as is human nature!

And one wonders also at the, I think, quite honest babbling of such authors to the effect that their novels are "true to life"—even in the bared teeth of a fact so self-evident and so unarguable as that writing can never be true to life.

No writing, I repeat, can be even remotely "true to life." For in writing we have a string of those arbitrary symbols termed words which one by one we interpret and so find out, approximately, what their author wished to tell us. He, in any case, remains our one source of information. But at every moment of living we have information (whether it be illusive or truthful) conveyed to us by our varied senses and by many

disconnected thoughts and by our memories and by an
emotion or two, all telling us about wholly different
matters simultaneously. No writer may hope to mimic
this hubbub, if but because his medium compels him to
tell us about one matter at a time.

He may vary his point of view, he may shift as speed-
ily as is permitted to his word-by-word medium from
one to another feature of living; but in dealing with
each and every feature, whether it be color or hunger
or movement or touch or envy or what not, he can but
hope, at the very best, to present it singly—which is
precisely what life never does.

Now at this instant I am conscious that my point is
a bit abstruse; that the hour lacks but twenty minutes
of lunch time; that many misguided persons have attempted the stream-of-consciousness method, which to
one reader, at any rate, conveys precisely nothing; that
Chesapeake Bay is beautiful; that the bill from the rug
cleaners was depressingly large; that I smell what I believe to be tomato pickle cooking; that my typewriter,
considering its age, has borne up uncommonly well;
that I too have been uncommonly lucky; that I like a
Martini plus dividend before lunch; that in Marjorie
Rawlings I lost, as well as a most dear friend, an irre-
placeable acquaintance; that she was especially proud
of her pickles; and that I had better get on with my
argument.

Of all these irrelated or but distantly allied matters,
I repeat, I am aware in one second's space; I know that
every second of our living is thus variously multi-con-

scious; and I infer that writing cannot ever, in any serious sense, be true to life.

Now the realist, of course and through a merciful necessity, edits and compresses his alleged truthfulness to life so as to get a story of sorts within book length. And here again is he false to his proclaimed model. Life does not ever edit or compress. Instead, life's multiconscious instants pass by interminably, each telling every one of us about a host of utterly irrelated or irrelevant matters simultaneously, and each defying record. No: it is not possible to render in words the complexity of even one moment of human consciousness, that consciousness which vibrates unceasingly through and which guides every human life; so that a book which purports to be truthful as to the life of its protagonist throughout several years could have been undertaken only by an author who was—well, what prudence limits me to describing as unreflective.

You see, there are a great many of these so-called realists about nowadays; and it does not pay to irritate the irrational.

Whensoever I speak of writers and of their quaint ways, though, it is with the mental reserve that, after all, I have not known many writers in the flesh with intimacy. With a number of them I have been on excellent terms. With dozens upon dozens of writers who were more or less famous in the 1920's, and whose fame oblivion has now dimmed and frayed, I used to forgather continually with, I believe, a shared pleasure.

But after all, in most cases, our yearlong acquaintance stayed superficial; and of their private lives I knew very little beyond that which they volunteered to tell me.

And this, heaven knows, was of a sufficiently intimate nature, upon divers evenings; yet I question if even prior to having named his choice of cocktails, a creative writer can be expected to speak concerning himself the truth uncolored. For if he be indeed an artist of any parts, then it is his profession to abridge and to re-arrange into symmetry and to heighten his narrative so as to make it more instantly impressive and more incisive. He avoids zealously, that is, being "true to life." To do this becomes with him a habit; his nature, as the tag runs, is subdued to what it works in; and in private discourse he soon learns to deal with himself fair-mindedly, in the same manner that in writing he deals with the universe at large.

Well, and as touches the most of my literary friends, each of them in his or her own province was an artist of parts; and in consequence their not unloquacious fragments of autobiography tended to become historical romances. Or at least I thought so even while I listened enjoyingly.

Yet in those bustling days, when the attempted suppression of one of my romances was still that which I may here be so pedantic as to term a *cause célèbre,* upon account of which all my hitherto neglected books and my future publishings also had of a sudden become vendible—and in this way had implicated me in continual business dealings which drew me to New York—

yet even then did I avoid going north any more frequently than circumstances compelled. The virtually
village-like New York in which as a very young man
I had frolicked, and in which as a newspaper reporter I
had passed some three more or less glamorous years, was
now at one with Arcadia; and I disliked forlornly and
fretfully its sprawling, ever-hurried successor. For but
one item, to subways or to taxis, as a substitute for the
more leisured comfort of the hansom cab, I was never
reconciled, nor do I hope to be.

So my visits to the city were kept too rare and too
abbreviated for me ever to rank as a member of the then
regnant intelligentsia who, in the New York of the
'twenties, were babbling in loud revolt against that, as
I still think, semi-fabulous monster, "the Puritan"; and
who most bellicosely and at their lungs' topmost reach
were advocating "trial marriages" and "free love" and
a many yet other evasions of prudery such as in Virginia the upper classes had learned long ago to enjoy
without talking about.

But during the early 1920's I met a fair assortment
of these, as I thought, somewhat childish Greenwich
Village people—and chief among them, gaunt and out
at elbows and forever garrulous John Macy, with whom
later on I was destined to find out that I shared rather
more in common than at this period I anticipated. But
of Macy I shall be speaking by-and-by, as one of my
collaborators in writing.

Moreover, I met, and I to a moderate extent became
friendly with, a number of then more famous authors

who flourished during this quaint era. And besides that, when in my native city *The Reviewer* began its fantastic and too brief career, then between 1921 and 1924 this small magazine drew toward Richmond a noble quota of these princes of literature—yes, including the great Mencken himself—along with a number of their female compeers, so that even in my partial anchoritism at Dumbarton Grange I saw much of many of them.

I was thus in those days by way of being almost intimate, for a while at any rate, with Frances Newman and Sinclair Lewis and Joseph Hergesheimer and Burton Rascoe and Hugh Walpole; Elinor Wylie and Carl Van Vechten I knew fairly well; and daily I became more familiar with Ellen Glasgow. And I at least met upon several occasions almost all of the other preeminent writers of this so multiform epoch, this now quite incredible decade of zest and of variousness in American letters between 1919 and 1929—when "the great depression" began, and included, I think, if not a depression of literary vigor, at least a diminishing of literary gusto.

Hereabouts, however, with a shock of surprise, the knowledge comes to me that not for a rather goodly while have I sampled many of the books of the more famous writers of that wonderful era of Mencken's supremacy in our literary affairs. The omission is due in chief, I know, to my once daily visited library's having been disordered and to every intent closed to me now for more than two years; but I question if an underlying unwillingness to find out exactly just how far beyond doubt these masterworks do or do not seem viable a quarter of a century after their deliverance to a delighted and a so painstakingly "sophisticated" reading public—"a small civilized minority," in Mencken's habitual phrase—may not buttress this omission.

I rather think it does. So many of these authors and authoresses then appeared to me so very important (even when, as with Willa Cather or Theodore Dreiser or Sherwood Anderson or Scott Fitzgerald, I for the life of me could not ever reach the point of reading their books completely) that to discover I nowadays find one or two of them to be worthy of oblivion—which at least possibly might be the outcome of my re-testing each of their masterpieces with my now more elderly eyes and my time-altered touchstones—would be depressive. The considerate oldster does not care thus roughly to destroy the illusions of youth, not even when the involved immaturity was wholly one's own and of that but relative callowness still possible to a provincially reared married man in his forties.

So I believe that, by and large, it might be wiser for me to recollect the leading literary figures of Mencken's era as they appeared to me during the 1920's rather than, just now at any rate, to go prodding about morbidly among the autographed relics of their time-dimmed grandeurs aligned upstairs in my library; and to re-read them, if at all, later on.

26

Remarks upon a Once Glorious Epoch

Imprimis, though, in virtually everything which Mencken published I, in those days, delighted. In private one might make bold to esteem him both as a literary and social critic more than often to be wrong—or childish even, or it might be just slightly pig-headed—in his estimate of this or of the other affair or person. But the magnificent vigor and vividness with which always the man presented his chosen point of view, no matter what might be his theme, resulted almost always in a work of dramatic art which you savored with enjoyment.

Think what you might, whether before or after the performance, there at the moment was no denying this H. L. Mencken was putting on a rousing good show. So that temporarily his æsthetic or political or social rightness or wrongness did not seem, to me at least, to be of weight; and I no more wanted to pause and argue about them than I would care to interrupt a fine performance of *Hamlet* by rising to protest that I did not believe in ghosts.

There in brief has been, and I think there can be, but one Mencken. He, in American letters, had no predecessor; his throne stays unfilled; and to my partial eyes a befitting heir is not visible among the several younger men who stand more than willing to succeed him as the monarch of a literary era.

Yes, and a monarch so thrifty that throughout his now semi-fabulous reign he elected to dispense with a court jester; and himself furnished for all his vassals a glut of fun continuously and offhand. I am proud to have served under His Majesty.

But of Mencken as he appeared to me in those days, the days of his noontide glory, I have written at some length in a tiny volume called *Some of Us*.

And therein also did I discourse as to Sinclair Lewis, to whom I now revert because, short only of Mencken, I take Sinclair Lewis to be the most amply characteristic author whom this era produced. They both of them, I mean, made it their business in life throughout the 1920's to "debunk"—here to employ with a large unwillingness that loathsome but unsynonymed word—pretty much every aspect of their times' contemporary life in the United States. And not many of its more grossly popular standards did the pair of them leave untottery for that while.

Lewis I had known, and I had liked heartily, both

as a person and as a youngster in whose genius I put faith, some two years prior to his spectacular success with *Main Street*. I was, I believe, when Hal Lewis— for I never called him "Red"—became famous almost overnight, one of the very few living persons who had read each of his five earlier novels, and who already possessed inscribed and autographed copies of them.

Well, and the general conception of *Main Street*, which I had heard all about of course from its not unduly taciturn writer when I read the novel's uncompleted typescript at the Rockbridge Alum Springs, and prompted a few changes in it, during the summer of 1919, appeared to me a deal better than was its final printed expression in the autumn of 1920. I enjoyed, that is, parts of this book far more than I did a vast quantity of its other parts. I thought the novel too long, and the writing of it straggly. Nor, it was an odd thing, saving only myself could I ever find anybody, not even at the height of the book's fame, who had read actually all of *Main Street*. It was the general conception of the book—the impairments wrought by the unconquerable smug "village virus" of small town life—which, as we say, caught on and became proverbial.

Babbitt, though, I admired almost unreservedly. But after *Babbitt* and after *Arrowsmith* (to which, just somehow, I did not warm over-enthusiastically), why, but then, to my judgment, Lewis rather too often for his own good as a writer resorted consciously to what he termed "whoring"—by which he referred to no bedroom activities, not hereabouts at least, but meant the rapid and facile writing of mediocre tales which his being famous enabled him to sell at a handsome rate to this or the other periodical. It was his notion, as he assured me more than once, that a practised author could do this whensoever he elected, and then, in his novels, return at will to writing in his best vein.

I did not argue about the matter. But nowadays I am quite firmly persuaded that the career of Sinclair Lewis disproved this notion. And, at any rate, I thought that *Mantrap* and *The Man Who Knew Coolidge* were almost unadulterated "whoring" in book form, and that in *Elmer Gantry*, an exaggeration which, by and large, I enjoyed, there was a great deal meritorious of the same Scriptural epitome.

Yet in *Dodsworth*, that novel which resulted—ultimately—from the wreck of his happiness with his first wife, Hal Lewis did produce, as lately as in 1929, what seemed to me the very best of all his books. Nor do I know of any more remunerative literary contrast than to compare *Dodsworth* with *Half a Loaf*, that so different, yet how much more than excellent novel (as I thought at least when it appeared in 1931), which Grace Hegger Lewis based upon her own and, so do I suspect, perhaps more accurate version of this tragedy.

Shortly after its climax I had the unhappy privilege of talking separately with each of its principals as to the causes of their divorce—or rather, upon both occasions I was talked to, at some length. And each of my annunciators, howsoever indignant as to what the speaker had been expected to put up with, and simply could not stand for one minute longer, why, but each of them as yet, or so did it seem to me, was quite plainly still more than half in love with the other.

They got over it, of course, in a world not over favorable to the immortalness of romance; and Lewis in fact was already remarried, to handsome and affable, gynarchic Dorothy Thompson. But even so, at this time, when I recollected the mutually adoring and impecunious and so proudly blissful young couple assured as to their ultimate conquest together of wealth and famousness and of the world in general, that couple whom I had known briefly a few years earlier, in the green wilderness of the Rockbridge Alum, why, but then I drew my own highly moral conclusions, in the very best Biblical vein of the Preacher, the son of David, King of Jerusalem, as to what being famous and wealthy may, after all, amount to.

Yes, and this morbid train of thought was revived when toward the end of March 1941, Hal Lewis of a sudden appeared in St. Augustine, and when among the cluttered and gaudy eighteen-eightyish splendors of the Hotel Ponce de Leon, I passed a far more than saddening evening with him. He by this time was divorced from his second wife; and he could talk about nothing whatever consecutively except to tell me over and over again the unhandsome details of how very badly he had been treated by some young actress or another upon whom, throughout the last several months at least, he had centered his affections. She but that week had discarded him, as I remember matters, in Miami; and I found him, in the most kindly terms which I can now think of offhand, to be maudlin over the young so-and-so's ungratefulness after all he had done for and had spent upon her.

He went northward early the next morning, pausing in Jacksonville, where, the day being Saturday, he unexpectedly entered the Jewish Temple and addressed the congregation upon the topic of America's giving yet more strenuous aid to Great Britain in the Second World War, opposing any such course with vigor. And in Jacksonville also, later in the same day, he declared he had been swindled out of $160 by a chance acquaintance first encountered there at a wayside tavern, in, as it happened, the bar room. Lewis had the man arrested, and then, overnight, continued his way north without appearing in court against the accused.

Well, and after that, as it happened, I never any more saw Sinclair Lewis. I grant, though, I did not desire to see him again. The Hal Lewis whom I had known and had been fond of, and in whose genius I had invested a prophetic faith some twenty-odd years earlier, had been transformed by his famousness far too utterly and far beyond recognition.

Nor after having plodded through *Ann Vickers*, did I ever chance to read any of his later books, for all that

I do remember having made a half-hearted endeavor to dispose of *Gideon Planish*.

Now, hereabouts, it occurs to me that this perilous notion of an author's being able to produce consciously inferior work for the immediate benefit of his bank account, and then at will to revert to writing his best, was harbored also by Joseph Hergesheimer. And for an odd reason, Hergesheimer did, so to speak, get away with it to perfection throughout a number of years, during which he contributed to the *Saturday Evening Post* those flamboyant stories of the quite simply dreadful goings-on of the idle rich, stories which their author frankly granted to be unworthy of republication; and yet, meanwhile, wrote some of his most excellent and most beautiful books.

The explanation, I think (as indeed I have pointed out in *Some of Us*), was that, just somehow, if Hergesheimer wrote as to contemporary life, then the results—to my finding, at least—tended to become flimsy and unimportant. (*Linda Condon* I took to be that axiomatic exception which proves every general rule.) But whensoever he turned to what he has called "the simpler loveliness of the past," then Hergesheimer almost always, and again just somehow, became a necromancer; and his magic, with ease and ever bountifully, evoked an America which it well may be did not ever quite exist, but which, even so, stayed none the less delightful to read about.

And so for one, I accepted this magic-working joyously without any Gradgrindian quibbles. For the creative verbal artist, after all, does not write upon a witness stand under the customary oath as to any uncustomary and antisocial truth-speaking.

It remains to me an undying regret that in this same *Some of Us* I should have included a mere mention of the name of Carl Van Vechten, whom I knew fairly well and liked completely, and from whose books I had derived varied and droll pleasures. If only, I reflect, instead of having felt it my duty to list a commentary upon Willa Cather, each of whose masterworks I have always had the ill taste to find tedious and third-rate, if only I had but included, as one of my book's decreed ten sections, a brief dissertation upon this how far more congenial author of *Peter Whiffle* and of *The Blind Bow Boy*—why, but in that event I could have dilated, and never so instructively, upon the quaint Age of Mencken's fond delight in being shocked, when this semi-sinister Van Vechten first began to publish novels, by the man's naughtiness, and in being edified by his sophistication.

For that, in those golden days, was a word to conjure with among us of the small civilized minority. We did not know, perhaps, precisely what "sophistication" meant. But, like "Mesopotamia," it was a most comfortable word in which one found large moral support. And we did know that this sophistication was nowhere present among our despised booboisie, our Bible belters, our wowsers, our rev. clergy, our campus critics, our noble swine, our merchants of palpable bosh, and, in brief, among all such benighted persons as did not read religiously and every month the *American Mercury* as that revered magazine was then being edited by H. L. Mencken and George Jean Nathan.

Well, and nowadays, of the aforetime famous writers whom I once knew more or less intimately, Ellen Glasgow and Frances Newman and Elinor Wylie and Sinclair Lewis and Hugh Walpole and Joseph Hergesheimer, all are dead. Carl Van Vechten and Burton Rascoe alone survive; and each of them, for this or the other reason, has ceased to publish any more books. Our era is ended.

And so, to my personal melancholic finding, the golden age of Mencken's supremacy and all its former glories really do seem, nowadays, to be quite at one with the golden age of Saturn and that throng of Titans who once animated it in a haze of no longer important legends. They have become myths viewed with incuriousness.

And for the rest, now that time and change and death have so variously estranged from me all these notabilities of the 1920's, it is pleasing to reflect that with none of them did I part in bitterness. Accuracy whispers, to be sure, that Hugh Walpole disrupted forever our then almost ten years old friendship upon account of a jesting reference to him (which I still know to have been wholly kindly and veracious) in a note, written by me, to Frances Newman, after this had been printed in a collection of her correspondence in the autumn of 1929. Nor did Elinor Wylie ever forgive me after hearing that I, who had been loud-lunged in praise of her first two prose romances, had then made bold, with whatsoever attempted privateness, not to adulate her *Orphan Angel.*

Yet, in each instance my acquaintance was dropped, if not tacitly, at least without any very much conversational abuse of my abominable behavior, even according to the reports of our joint literary friends, who most certainly would never have spared me the worst somewhat augmented. And in each case did I condone with complacence enough that which seemed to me, I admit, an outburst of infantile vanity.

The thought occurs hereabouts, as a deplored reflection upon human nature, that whenever a friend is lost (otherwise than through death, which even prior to the funeral raises about death's victim a beguiling haze), then you become aware with a sad soonness of a number of reasons for not, after all, becoming heartbroken over the affair. There, in fact, enters into your all-decorous regret a sneaking element of relief. The friend has departed out of your life and presumably forever; you are sorry about this; but, at least, he has taken along with him his faults and his more or less fretting idiosyncracies of which no breathing person lacks a fair competence. You are not going to be bothered with them any more. So by the eye of optimism there is always a bright facet or two to be found in a shattered friendship.

Of Hugh Walpole—for a precise example—I was fond with sincerity and with gratitude also, because, during his first lecture tour of the United States, in 1919 and 1920, he had spoken repeatedly in praise of my writings. Of his own accord, and when I was yet a stranger to him, he, who was then at the height of his American fame, had likewise published, in the *Yale Review,* a remunerative article concerning my books, belauding them liberally; and so had increased their sales to an appreciable extent, at a time when every visiting British author was hearkened to with reverence. For that I remained grateful. For that I am still grateful. And I delighted in his personal charm.

When I first knew him, Hugh was in his thirties; his health as yet remained excellent; and his appearance was handsome. His manner was uniformly ingratiating; he brimmed over with enthusiasm, as to this, that or the other matter, boyishly; and he talked always entertainingly, even with an informal eloquence. He did speak rather often, it is true, as to the various exalted and celebrated persons with whom he was hand and glove, so it seemed, all over the world; but that which he narrated concerning them, to me in my confessed provincialism, I found of applaudable interest. He appeared, moreover, to like everybody in those days; and as to his own books he spoke with an engaging gay modesty—he who later on began so feverishly to accredit to malice and to personal enmity any and all not wholly flattering comment upon whatever he published.

I could not but be pleased, too, that he urged me, deserting temporarily my family and my smug suburban living, to visit England as his guest, so that he might present me to all the local nobility and literati—"whom I really ought to know, and with whom I would get on famously"—nor was I unamused or untouched by his almost casual offer to pay my expenses throughout the trip. For why, pray, shouldn't he, Hugh demanded, when he nowadays, as he told me with a childlike gusto, was making ever and ever so much more money than he quite knew what to do with?

In brief, I found this effusive and affectionate youngster (as he then seemed to me) to be almost wholly attractive. And I still like to remember the nine years or thereabouts of our amity.

To the other side, for a number of his male friends, or even for many but newly made male acquaintances, a tête-à-tête with Hugh Walpole had its awkwardness. If you shared his inclinations, of course, why, then well and good. One has no call to reprove them over-virtuously, now that these special tastes are regarded rather more widely as a mental illness than as a criminal offense. But if you did not share his inclinations, then were you far too likely to find a continual need to remind him of this circumstance a continual nuisance.

As did a large host of his well-wishers who, like me,

were no longer juvenile nor pre-eminent in any An-
tinous-like beauty. I can recall, for instance, how Mere-
dith Nicholson, the Hoosier novelist, then time-wiz-
ened and a good bit farther on than I was toward the
mortician's, once inquired of me—as I thought, for a
former diplomat, somewhat naively—in regard to this
semi-public secret:—

"But whatever on earth is the matter, anyhow, with
that fellow Hugh Walpole? I had just met him the
other day, and I thought I liked him tremendously. But
the very first minute we were left together he began
acting like a lunatic."

And when I had replied with verbal discretion, yet
with sufficing plainness, then Nicholson made a slight
whistling noise of genuine surprise, and he said:—

"I see. I think it's a great pity in a fine chap like
that."

I agreed with him.

And, besides this drawback, my admiration for
Hugh's books was limited. They appeared to me to be
reasonably good in their fashion, but it was not a fashion in which I delighted. Yet in talking with him, of
course, or in writing to thank him for that copy of his
latest book which had come to me adorned with a personal inscription and an autograph, I could hardly, no,
not decently, avoid a polite perjuring or two. And he
produced so very many books, so very, very rapidly, during the nine years of our friendship, that my powers of
exaggeration were strained over and yet over again in

eulogy of each brand-new volume's, as I vexedly thought at bottom, exceedingly mild merits. I confess here that, after he once broke with me, I never bothered to read a book by Hugh Walpole. And I found it a relief not any longer to have to make this, to me, unrewarding investment of spare moments.

With Elinor Wylie the case was far otherwise. To her poetry I extended a temperate approval, because it seemed to me excellent poetry, even now that my days for caring deeply about anybody's poetry were over. Concerning *Jennifer Lorn* and *The Venetian Glass Nephew,* however, my enthusiasm had few limits when these romances appeared; and in common with Carl Van Vechten, I babbled as to them in blurb after blurb. As concerned the *Nephew,* indeed, I went far beyond Carl's more temperate liking.

But *The Orphan Angel* I found impenetrable, nor to this day have I ever read all of it. And I said that I thought it to be not quite so good as its predecessors, speaking thus over-rashly to, of all persons, another professional writer, who of course repeated this adverse judgment posthaste to Elinor Wylie, as was then the manner of us littérateurs in delightedly stirring up trouble among our fellow practitioners during those evil years of yore. Nowadays, in our present apocalypse of American letters, so do they tell me, all practising authors love one another even as did the members of that yet other reformed menagerie foretold in the eleventh chapter of the vision of Isaiah the son of Amoz.

Well, and the temperament of Elinor Wylie being what it was, she never so much as dreamed of forgiving me this tepid dispraise, inasmuch as her touchiness was beyond instant belief, alike as to her writings, every least line of them, and her personal loveliness also. The most tiny hint that either her genius or its corporeal clothing in any most tiny feature fell short of perfection, would arouse straightway, whether secludedly or in public, a storm of tears and beget an everlasting rancor. For of her associates she required continuous flattery; yet lacking it, she did not ever so far condescend as to sulk. She, instead, "made scenes" in the more tempestuous manner of a tragedienne of yesterday's school, and she at once, so to speak, "cut up" with the high unrestrainedness of a Mrs. Leslie Carter or a Sarah Bernhardt. You, in her company, had thus an uneasy feeling of smoking rather more than was good for you in a gunpowder magazine.

Yes; I admired Elinor Wylie wholly, both as an author and as an actually all-beautiful woman; I cherished even a latent respect for the mad stubbornness with which, as an oblation to perfection, she chose to live in a perpetual semi-blindness rather than to wear glasses in public; but at that, in 1926, I faced quite resignedly my enforced need to revere her wonderfulness henceforward from a reassuring distance. And I revere it no less fondly, do you let me add, today also in recollection.

I do not know why a majority of authors, or at any

rate, almost all whom I have known as persons, should be thus tetchy. I can but attribute it to our trade's underlying self-suspicion of, at least possibly, being about a childish employment in a world of adults; and to a consequent, ever fretful desire to be justifying this employment, howsoever speciously.

Now hereabouts, at worst, I have been tolerably honest. I have confessed over and yet over again that to me this business of writing has been at bottom sheer pleasure-seeking. I for that matter have devoted, in *Straws and Prayer-Books,* an entire volume to preaching from the text that, "The literary artist labors primarily to divert himself"; and for this sacred but unpopular truth, I have shown a befitting reverence in my own conduct always. I, as a writer, have made bold to dabble in no high social or philosophic or moral causes. I have diffused no reforms, no fault-findings. My fellow creatures, as I found them, have entertained me too amusingly and too tenderly for me to wish them especially changed. I have written, in brief, each of my books, because for one reason or another, it was the book which at that particular time I wanted to write, and because I enjoyed writing it.

And so, when people have been at pains to announce they did not enjoy the results, their grave, or in no few cases their frenzied, reproofs have seemed to me upon the same plane as finding fault with a sewing machine, because it does not transmit radio programs, or as disparaging a straw hat for being, virtually, as unpleasing to the palate as are the more popular breakfast foods. The maker of each article, one can but reply to this sort of criticism, designed it for a serviceableness somewhat other than that of which a lack is being lamented.

Yet whenever my books do prove to have pleased this or the other outspoken reader, then I confess to an elatedness, which, in part, is a vainglorious sense of benefaction, but above all, is a sense of congeniality, that none too frequent perception of having encountered a person whose tastes are pretty much the same as your own. Because these books also have pleased me.

I speak, it should be observed, in the past tense. My books, one by one, have pleased me, and very cordially, through the enjoyment which I got out of each one of them at the time it was being written. I am still grateful to each one of them for this enjoyment, but for that only. Out of reading any of my completed and printed books I by-and-by (in common, from an economic standpoint, with a regrettably huge host of my fellow creatures) can derive no pleasure whatever; but, rather, just that half wistful, half puzzled emotion with which we regard a photograph of ourselves perpetrated when we were younger.

"And that is what I used to be like!" we then feel without joyousness. For no matter how fantastic or how handsome or how hideous the photograph may seem to us, we, who no longer at all resemble it, know we confront a dead person.

Well, and an author, it is my experience, comes by-and-by, if only he lives long enough, to regard his own books, which so variously reflect his ideals at the time when each book was written, in very much this same fashion.

27

Is of Two Whom I Admired Dubiously

Howeveʀ! and with such gratifyingly congenial persons as but now I spoke of—with persons whose tastes in writing were pretty much the same as mine—I have been so lucky as to share the intimacy of collaboration upon more than one occasion, it here occurs to me. And thereupon my thoughts fondly and yearningly hark back to Guy Holt, with whom for well-nigh ten years I collaborated as thoroughly as did the Grimm brothers or the Goncourt brothers with each other, or as Beaumont with Fletcher, or as Gilbert with Sullivan, without, in my case, my co-laborer's ever being acknowledged with any explicitness.

Holt was throughout this period the literary editor of the publishing firm of Robert M. McBride & Company; and when I first heard from him, in the April of 1915, he had but newly turned twenty-three. This youthfulness may well have accounted for the enthusiasm with which he then accepted an oddly entitled novel, *The Rivet in Grandfather's Neck,* after that story had been rejected by I know not how many publishers beyond the fact that they in numerousness exceeded thirteen.

I met him in that same April; and we, as they say, took to each other at once.

But our actual collaboration began in 1917, with a sort of a something that I called *Beyond Life;* and this partnership continued unbroken throughout no less than ten books and booklets, to every one of which Guy Holt contributed with a prodigality that would have well justified his being named as their co-author. For, in those days, I used to discuss with him each one of my books before it was written, a thing which I have never even attempted with any other person; and then to keep on with our discussion while the book was being put together; and afterward to resume this debating when my first version had been typed and he had read it in, as it were, its embryo. And all the while his comments would be tonically scathing, and his suggestions endless, alike for re-wording and for added or changed scenes and for new turns of incident as well as for excisions. And all the while, too—or at any rate, for the most part—I, with a sober rejoicing, followed his advice, because it so clearly made for improvement.

That we both enjoyed this collaboration, I know. The debating of all conceivable points as to each book became a sort of friendly tussle, with both of us upon our mettle and no holds barred, so that our minds worked more nimbly in the glow of encounter with an unsparing adversary. *Beyond Life* and *Jurgen* and *Figures of Earth, Straws and Prayer-Books* and *The High Place* and *The Silver Stallion*—of all these I would probably have been guilty in any case. But except for Guy Holt, I suspect, there is in no one of them any page which would have taken quite the form in which it was printed. He contributed, it may be, no paragraph, and perhaps hardly a complete sentence, as it now stands in any one of these volumes; but he altered, and more handsomely, the shape and the texture of each book through his superior and incessant fault-finding with my first and my second and I know not how many other versions of each book.

Of his out-and-out additions to my texts I appear to have kept but one tangible record. I recall that in *The Silver Stallion* he invented the entire story of Gonfal, somewhat as Thomas Beer presented me with the germ of Guivric of Perdigon's misadventures, which Beer had happened to encounter in Sicilian demonology. Yes, and I can yet identify sundry passages in *Jurgen* and in *The High Place* which Holt's denunciations thereof induced me to change entirely, in accord with his personal and, as I thought, far better notion as to how these passages ought to run; but of his bulkiest contribution to *Beyond Life* I have still the first typescript.

It was completed by him, I find, upon 5 January 1917, and it contains four extra-large, very closely-typed pages of protest against what he took to be heretical and misleading and inconsistent, or even downright silly, in this interminable monologue attributed to John Charteris, which, in the book's first form, must have continued uninterrupted to the book's end. But Guy Holt's depreciation of what he assumed to be the haphazard dicta voiced by Charteris—in this prologue to the not as yet completed Biography of the Life of Manuel—I thought far too common-sensible to let slip; and so did the last chapter become a duologue throughout which I (with a growing self-admiration) put into my own mouth the exact protest which Holt had filed. Here and there I changed it verbally with a free hand; but the gist and most of the wording of all that which in this final chapter I am supposed to be saying, with so much of sound logic and of good sense, in reply to Charteris was said first by an affably sadistic Guy Holt, as this typescript proves more than amply.

Well, and I am certain that with better luck our collaborating would have continued for some eight years longer than it did, and would have been ended only by Holt's premature and sudden death in the April of 1934. But a need to exalt, or at any rate to make more sonorous, his official rank in the publishing world impelled Guy Holt to leave McBride's in the early summer of 1926—just after we had finished and brought out *The Silver Stallion*—and to share in founding the John Day Company, as a full-fledged partner therein. So, with deep sorrow, did I then face the loss of my invaluable collaborator.

Yet as a token of good will, I wrote for Holt's new firm *The Music from Behind the Moon,* to be their first published volume. And this brief story was destined to remain the very last one upon which Guy Holt and I worked together. None of my later books did he ever see or debate with me until after it was published, for all that our personal friendship stayed warm and unaltered until of a sudden his death had severed it overnight.

When I informed Holt that *Something About Eve,* the first bit of writing which within ten years I had done without his advisement's aid, had gone forth to the printers, I find him answering as to this as yet unseen story,—

"You will forgive me, I trust, if I look upon it always as a creature that has not properly been spanked into existence; and feel an aggrieved sense of loss that over this new book of yours there has been no exchange of discourtesies between us."

And here were sentiments I shared utterly. Throughout the remainder of Guy Holt's life I felt forlornly as to every book I completed after 1927 that it would have been improved if only his tonic carpings could have helped, as he phrased matters, to spank it into existence.

Now to this day I can but guess at why his so vivid and vibrant talents—and as I think, his genius—took form in no book which he wrote completely. For the man loved good writing. He had all the gifts which were needed to achieve it and to have ranked him, so do I believe, among the most admirable of contemporary authors. But not ever did he find the time in which to exercise these gifts continuously and to the full.

In chief, I think, this was because he enjoyed too numerous avocations, in the form of social gatherings, and of friendly drinking bouts (though he drank sparingly and but to the point of a slightly garrulous exhilaration), and of divers not uncomplaisant young women, and always of talk for talk's sake, and of yet a great many other amenities from any at all frequent indulgence in which a writer who views authorship as an exercise of art rather than as a source of income is debarred by the stubborn fact that a day contains but twenty-four hours. So does each member of this besotted small brotherhood (who regard one another, you may note, with a fraternal lack of adulation) need to stint the normal pleasures of life; and he gets, in exchange for this sacrifice, the time wherein to achieve the prolonged and lonely labors, the unending toil, from out of which, or to my experience at least, he extracts an illogical contentment.

Well, and it was a contentment which Guy Holt did not at bottom desire; and it, in fact, is a perverted form of hedonism I am not defending; yet I grieve that, or so it seems to me, his gifts were squandered upon enjoying his life through more rational channels, and thus stayed without any permanent fruitage. I am not questioning, though, that he may have made by far the better personal bargain through living, if a whit irresponsibly perhaps, yet always more normally than is permitted to creative writers, throughout his allotted brief span.

Then there was another collaboration of sorts between John Macy and myself, when we assembled together the volume of selections entitled *Between Dawn and Sunrise*. And if in John Macy's companionship also I found pleasure, after once my narrow-mindedness had grown accustomed to the resolute Bohemianism of his daily ways, yet in him, too, did I find a provoker of aggrieved wonderment. For although he wrote not uncopiously, and for the most part it was a praiseworthy enough output, in the form of literary or of semi-literary articles, yet always his talents—or as I thought, just as in Guy Holt's case, his native genius—got never any full exercise, and his masterworks stayed unwritten. Always John Macy was going to attend to them, oh, but more than amply, by-and-by. Meanwhile he enjoyed talking about them—as he, indeed, enjoyed talking about pretty much every matter under the sun, except only his wife.

Here we touch tragedy. World-famous Anne Sullivan Macy, as you may or may not recall nowadays, had won public acclaim by teaching a blind deaf-mute to read and to talk and to write rather remarkably mediocre books. Yet was Anne Sullivan Macy in her private life, and to her husband's ruin, a marked example of the unpleasantness which may be brought about by an accomplished and strident woman under the battle

flag of irreproachable motives. So, when Macy had left
her after a brief while of marriage—as, it was his con-
tention, any other unparalyzed male would have done
rather than submit to stay a minor component of Anne
Sullivan Macy's entourage, in daily contrast to her
more profitably and so blatantly publicized, pathetic
blind pupil and remunerative show-piece—why, but
then his wife, who was by more than eleven years his
senior, declined to divorce him, because she considered
divorces immoral. Or so, at any rate, Anne Sullivan
Macy declared unshakably.

That left her nominal husband foot-loose at thirty
or thereabouts; and, for the last twenty years or so of his
virtual homelessness, they never met again. And it was
the tragedy of his life, so did John Macy believe, or
at most times anyhow, that this pig-headed paragon
would not ever leave him free to marry another woman,
and to settle down into domestic living and the beget-
ting of legitimate children.

It is true that the identity of this other woman tended
to vary. Here was a circumstance which may, it is possible, have strengthened the moral principles of Anne
Sullivan Macy and have increased her deafness toward
those frenzied and repeated appeals for a divorce which
were presented to her, every year or so, by John Macy's
delegates. Yes; one in fairness, and with whatsoever
unwillingness, must weigh her side of the matter. When
your husband himself appears to be thus various-minded
as to your preferred successor, then a so rigidly virtuous
woman may very well, and with some show of logic,

hold that, if but simply for his own good, there had best not be any successor made legal and possibly permanent.

I do not know anything about the workings of the mind of a virtuous woman, or for that matter, of any woman's mind. I know only that upon one occasion but a little while before his death, which occurred of a sudden in the August of 1932, John Macy said wistfully and, as I think, with complete truthfulness,—

"I have never hated but one person in my life, and I had the misfortune to marry her."

Well, and nowadays I myself believe that an emotion not far from hatred was justified. I believe that Anne Sullivan Macy, smugly and callously, ruined the life of a man of latent and all-amiable genius. But she did this, it is my yet further belief, not by her stubbornness in refusing him a decent freedom and a possible home, but by providing for him too much sympathy and over-convenient excuses. All those who knew John Macy and his personal perennial charm (as it was my privilege to do for some fourteen years) could not but sympathize so far with his unhopeful position and his enforced vagabondage as to condone an occasional excess in the way of self-comforting. If he now and then drank a bit too much or entered into unlegalized sexual activities, why, but you felt—and so did he—that, after all, he had every conceivable extenuation.

Here was, in short, a year-long dilemma in which even the most self-controlled of men who, like John Macy, was as yet saddled with virileness, endowed with magnetism, and gifted with the profile of an heroic tragedian, would be endangered daily. But, above all, nocturnally.

It was, I grant you, very much the same predicament in which Theodore Dreiser (although to my thinking, he was spared the pitfall of personal charm) was then living with a fair show of tranquilness, and in defiance of which Dreiser had set to work and was producing his, to my finding, unexhilarant novels equably. But John Macy had about him no such stolidness. He, to the contrary, delighted secretly, I believe, in being fate's victim. He delighted visibly in being an artist, a Socialist, an agnostic, a true-blue Bohemian, and a rebel against every known genteel convention; so that he dressed always for the part with exuberantly flowing Windsor ties and the most informal yet other habiliments conceivable.

He delighted likewise to talk, and to talk quietly, with a staid brilliance, but to talk endlessly, by the hour, about literature and literature's makers and about all matters connected therewith howsoever remotely, such as, for extreme examples, the writing which you were doing and the writing which he also was about to do next week at latest, or, at any rate, during the following month. So that, for the life of you, you could not but enjoy being with and listening to him, or help being sorry for him. It, somehow, was like observing a lonesome child very resolutely at play.

The sole yet fatal trouble was that this continuous

enactment of being fate's victim and of being an artist
and a social rebel, &c., this continuous talking over a
fairly moderate amount of beverages until after midnight, this continuous exercise of his amiability alike in
conversation and in bedrooms, all this, while hurtless
enough in each several item, all this—just as I have
noted in the case of Guy Holt—consumed far too many
hours in a day which possessed but twenty-four of them.
So John Macy's writing, done at, I think, half-grudged
and not over-long intervals between these avocations,
suffered perforce.

His half-dozen or so books, and, in particular, *The
Spirit of American Literature,* are sound enough, to my
finding, so far as they go. Yet is this going not far beyond commonplaceness. His writing does not often, and
indeed does not ever, rise to the levels which—still, with
no backing whatsoever more valid than is my own personal notion—I believe the literary gifts of John Macy,
in quiet and prolonged seclusion, might handsomely
have attained.

About this I cannot ever be certain. I am wholly certain, though, that in the lives of divers, liberal-minded
women, who did not overrate the negative virtue of continence, he created pleasure and affection; and I, now
and then, believe that to enkindle happiness upon this
planet may after all, in the unpeevish eyes of omniscience, very well appear a feat more praiseworthy than
is the creation of an enduring book.

It, in fact, to the reflective, seems quite possible that
Jehovah, as being nowadays the one living author as-

sured of remaining a classic, does not keep rigorously abreast with each and every contribution to latter-day American literature; or much bother about books so extremely remote from and alien to His own period of productiveness in romantic fiction.

And at any rate—still, just as in the case of Guy Holt —I am not denying that, with but one so brief mortal life at his disposal, John Macy may have made the best bargain obtainable through enjoying that life to the full, small extent permitted him; and through being, if somewhat futile, yet almost always lovable. My common-sense, howsoever limited, is yet lively enough to deter me from any such zealotism in art's behalf. Art, my common-sense remarks invidiously, has had more than enough of your intermeddling.

And besides, as I have suggested, besides, if only just now and then, I am not certain but that being lovable is a more rare and a more rewarding, as it, beyond doubt, seems a more charitable performance than is the ultimate revealing of one's literary genius to the stilted and verbose plaudits of tomorrow's schoolmasters and the reluctant attention of their pupils.

28

Discourses upon the Impiety of Art

THESE two men, then, loom foremost among my memories of a number, a large number, of acquaintances who were endowed, I am certain, with rather large literary talents which they never developed. The names of these various other persons need not here concern us, for they would mean to you nothing—which equally must be nowadays, for that matter, the significance in general of the names of Guy Holt and John Macy, of whose gay and ardent personalities exist, tangibly upon earth, only their tombstones.

But in each instance I am afraid I rather nagged all these persons, at one or another time, about their omission to be writing a sincerely self-expressive book or two, if only because of my Scots blood, which abhors wastefulness of anything whatever, even of a possession so personally unremunerative, in the long run, as is an ability to create distinguished literature.

For dimly it is my superstition that this ability is

195

an innate gift received from some supernatural Somebody other than Jehovah; and that the recipient owes it to this Somebody (as to whose name or nature I dare hazard no guess) to develop the gift ungrudgingly. Not to do this, I feel to be shirking, also, that trueness to one's own self which, by way of Polonius, Shakespeare commends in every known list of familiar quotations.

By Somebody, I have said, other than Jehovah. I would not suggest, not explicitly, that the begetter of all art is Satan. I mean merely that I cannot imagine any level-headed and equitable deity's inflicting at birth upon any one of his creatures, who is expected henceforward to obey the Decalogue and the yet other a many ethic or legal regulations of our present-day at least nominally Christian orderings, an artist's temperament. Because to serve and to cultivate the fruitage of that temperament and, at the same time, to respect always these various orderings, appears simply and flatly, whatsoever we might prefer, not possible. So as a communicant, one would rather not think that the Lord God of Battles Himself creates the "born" artist, who thereby is made likewise a predestined law-breaker, and as such is punishable with a host of post-mortem torments. Omniscience could hardly miss the fact that a true artist must, and that of necessity he will, attend to his art first, and to his merely human or moral obligations second.

Here is a doctrine not popular among sound citizens, nor does the wise creative artist profess it with ostentation. He, instead, does but honor this doctrine with the commingled devoutness and discretion and secrecy of an Early Christian attending divine worship in the catacombs beneath Nero's Rome.

It followed that I involved myself in some little obloquy not very long ago by pointing out that an innately gifted male author—by which I do not mean a man of large genius, not necessarily, but merely a person born predestinated to authorship—requires, and that he will inevitably make use of, whether with openness or hugger-mugger, an extra-legal number of women throughout the prime of his physical vigor, because these deviations from continence alike stimulate and sustain and enlarge his power to write. He thus needs in the developing of his writing an occasional change of women just as he needs now and then to change his typewriter ribbon. And he will secure, somehow, both of these changes at any cost, because to develop his writing is his main object in life.

Nobody who knew anything about writers disputed this, as I termed it with frankness, "wholly undesirable truth," or, indeed, would ever think of disputing it. But a spluttering number of highminded dunces were moved, forthwith, to resent in print this insult to a noble profession, this flagrant defence of immorality, this senile gloating over long-past lecheries, and—well, but I really do forget, just now, what other enormities they found in this casual statement of a fact which an ignoramus alone could deny.

Yet now I come to think of it, the most shrill and

sullen and uncondoning complaint was that I admitted I, myself, like everybody else, had indulged when young in some love-affairs; and that in my attempt to make clear the evolution of each and every known creative writer, I told how later on, just as all writers extort from such inevitable transactions profit, so had these affairs been utilized as the raw material of my various fictions.

Well, but for an author to grant in print that he has ever had any amorous dealings, or to record with gratitude their usefulness to him, is by many estimable if unadventurous-minded persons such as are the mainstay of book clubs and churchwork esteemed revolting. So the outlining of my remote youth's development led, exactly as I had been at pains to predict, "to my being accredited, among the obtuse, with an obtuse, boastful and repugnant, lewd egotism."

It stays puzzling to me, in passing, just how this notion could ever have come into being, that a writer should never admit, not with frankness, any sexual experience to have had a part in originating any of his books or to have figured in his life. For we confront here the sole, droll exception (at which I hinted a fair number of pages back) to an author's being permitted to play at harboring omniscience. This one exception is that, by the genteel, it is demanded he should always pretend that anything which his books may tell you as to love-affairs and the goal of every normal love-affair is an out-and-out invention contrived by a person who, through experience, does not know anything whatever about such matters. He must not ever grant in print that, in common with the run of all men, he has shared in such contortive spasms with enthusiasm and effusiveness.

Well, and this taboo, as goes its complete unaccountability, I cannot but rank with another ruling by the well-thought-of which I have lamented earlier, to the effect that no writer should ever allude in print to the more pleasing qualities of his wife during her lifetime. There seems to me, so do I confess with due humbleness, to exist no possible explaining of either one of these notions upon rational grounds. Yet to many, no doubt more acute if apparently rather dull-witted persons, each of these assumptions appears obvious; and in their thinking, for that matter, the affair takes on a smug tinge of morality.

All which reminds me that sincere creative writing, as I understand it, must remain always, not in the least inimical, but indifferent, to popular morals, which it will serve or which it will violate as may best suit the writer's requirements. And by sincere creative writing, I mean writing which develops unfalteringly the writer's innate gifts and his innate predilections, such as they may happen to be, and which thus remains always true to his actual personality. He endeavors, that is, to express himself without bothering about any of his fellow creatures' notions or their overlords, or about his own immediate secular overlords either. And, in his writing, he tries to create a world just such as he desires to rule as its god, controlling and making sport for himself with its inhabitants, without of necessity imitating the methods of building and populating a world which were instituted some while ago, so does my faith as an Episcopalian assure me, by Jehovah. The creative writer thus, in some sort, becomes Jehovah's rival practitioner.

And all this of course is no more true of the open and aboveboard romanticist than of the realist, because, as I already have had occasion to point out, the latter relentlessly and blatantly omits from his fancied world the guiding principle of that phenomenon, so omnipresent in our own flesh-and-blood world, which we term human nature. A realist can have no dealings whatever with human nature's quenchless and fantastic optimism without which no human beings can exist or would care to exist. He, in consequence, endeavors impiously to depict life from a standpoint whence, it is my conviction, no human being has ever been permitted to regard life and continue living. Whereas, with an equal impiety, does the romanticist display to us what in his opinion is the sort of world which, if only Jehovah had been a little bit more competent, would have been set agoing in the September of 4004 B.C.

By and large, then, the hypothesis does appear at least tenable that it is Satan who foists upon the "born" creative writer the ability and the need to be about a vocation thus doomed to be more or less gravely blasphemous. And it may be that all those among my acquaintances who, like Guy Holt and John Macy, possessed this ability, but who abstained from exercising it, displayed a wholly pious self-restraint when they evaded my pleas in the ungracious role, without my ever knowing it, of *advocatus diaboli*.

To the other side, let us remember that a truly Christian deity such as Jehovah Himself became but shortly after the Crucifixion, would weigh the circumstance that the creative writer, whatsoever his blasphemy, is very often (even though it be only a by-product of his hedonism) a benefactor of mankind, dispensing among his fellow creatures much laudable enjoyment. He writes, that is, for his own pleasure, selfishly, but that pleasure may prove contagious.

No author, for a venerable example, has ever parodied more flagrantly and consistently and unconscionably, or more gloriously, the actual nature and the normal orderings of the world he inhabited than did Charles Dickens. One can almost imagine Jehovah's regarding, say, Mr. Micawber or Mrs. Sarah Gamp or Sam Weller—and any number of yet other Dickens characters, beside whom mere behemoths and pleiosauri and dinosaurs become drably commonplace—with a vexed envy over the Lord God of Sabaoth's own failure to have created any such prodigious creatures. And yet, too, Jehovah would then be reflecting with an unavoidable chuckle, how very few if any other human beings, besides this impious outreacher of My utmost endeavors in the way of monsterdom, have ever disseminated anything like so much hurtless delight among such numerous millions!

So one cannot but think that, by the splendor of these benefactions to his fellow mortals, all the pettiness and the pig-headedness of Dickens' private life, and all his dealings with his unfortunate wife and with Ellen Ternan and so on, must have been wholly eclipsed in the eyes of divine justice. Yes; as his daughter, Kate Perugini, acknowledged with commingled affection and abhorrence, "My father was a wicked man—a very wicked man." For this Charles Dickens sinned freely, and he never dreamed of repentance, nor seemed to think any was called for. And yet, just somehow, one cannot but believe he was forgiven out of hand immediately after his death, upon account of his so prodigal largesse and ever-living legacies to his fellow beings.

I, at least, hope so. When I remember all the vivid and varied pleasures, if not always, as I have confessed, the inveterate pleasures, which during the last sixty and more years I have derived from the books of Dickens and from scores upon hundreds upon, it is possible, thousands of books by yet other persons, then, with a benevolent illogic, I hope that some such wholly unfair favoritism has been extended from above to each of their authors.

Most certainly, I reflect, should every one of these writers be listed as persons whom I still like with an abiding gratitude for the pleasure which they once gave me, a pleasure which is in no way concerned with my present-day sentiments toward re-reading their books; and yet merely to enumerate these writers here would extend the volume now in your hands beyond portableness.

That, in fact, is my trouble. I in one way or another, I in my time, have derived very many by-ends of enjoyment from my, upon the whole, rather uneventful living; and as befits fairness, I perforce stay grateful to the purveyor of each several enjoyment, no matter whether he, or perhaps she, be nowadays dead or estranged, or even if, as in some cases, the purveyor was not ever known to me as a definite personality.

I am still grateful, for but one instance, to the Mr. Hershey who first manufactured those cakes of milk chocolate which, for so numerous years, I devoured by the half-pound with gusto and no deplored aftermath, for all that today I never taste them or even note them upon sale anywhere. For the pleasure which this Mr. Hershey once afforded me in the prime of my digestion's intrepidity, I remain forever indebted, without recalling, if indeed I ever knew, his Christian name or his post-office address during that omnivorous era—and very certainly without knowing his present-day residence, inasmuch as I assume him to have been dead a great while since.

But, in that event, I hope he left earth for heaven, just as gratitude compels me to cherish the same aspiration concerning William Harrison Ainsworth, and Howard Pyle, and William Shakespeare, and Andrea

Solario, and sundry daughters of joy whom I knew transiently (but merely in a Biblical sense), and Hans Christian Andersen, and Victor Herbert, and H. Rider Haggard, and Thomas Alva Edison, and the primal distiller of apple brandy, and Gustave Moreau, and St. Paul of Tarsus, and Richard Mansfield, and that heaven-sent editor of Muscovite folk-lore, W. R. S. Ralston, M. A., and Minnie Maddern Fiske, and the inventor of the game of anagrams (which, such is my antiquity, I first played as "letters"), and Gilbert-and-Sullivan, and Theocritus, and Mother Goose—as to none of whom as persons do I know anything at all definite beyond the fact that, at odd times, they have each one of them made very much more pleasurable a portion of my existence.

And to a now incredible extent was this true, it here occurs to me, of Stephen Vincent Benét.

29

Concerning Another Fond Obligation

I AM here reminded, I repeat, of my unique indebtedness to Stephen Vincent Benét, among creative writers, alike in the way of pleasure and of profit. It was a debt which began, oddly enough, through his serving as a publisher's reader for Farrar & Rinehart when I first joined forces with that firm in 1938; and through John Farrar's sending to me, as one by one my romances got to him in typescript, Benét's report concerning each book.

I warmed to these reports, in part, because of their pervasively complimentary flavor, which flattered my self-complacence, but still more because of their, if now and then extreme, yet always intelligible and intelligent, fault-finding. Here for the first time since Guy Holt and I had collaborated on *The Music from Behind the Moon* in 1926, I felt, was I getting, from John

Farrar and Stephen Benét between them, an abundance of derogation at a season when I might profit by it.

We face here a writer's perpetual puzzle as to professional criticism—which, of necessity, reaches him after the concerned book has been printed. Its author may then find pointed out by never so many indubious Rhadamanthi his errors and his shortcomings, or it may be his worthlessness, or perhaps his enormities: and what present good can it do him, now that he lacks any power to remedy matters, with the book a finished product and beyond his control? At utmost he can but humbly resolve to avoid in his next publishing the faults which have damnified his current volume; but, even in this case, he upon reflection notes almost always that his more unlenient judges, howsoever infallible sounding, howsoever universally revered in bookdom, yet have contradicted one another by condemning blemishes which cannot conceivably co-exist. Which mentor, then, is he to respect henceforward?

An author fairly well known to me, for an example, was but the other day expressing perplexity over the circumstance that a leading critic had found his latest publication, which was a tiny volume of reminiscences, to be over petulant and plaintive, while another policeman of polite letters, no whit less eminent, deplored its being too smug and too boastful.

"And however on earth," quoth the bewildered writer, "can my poor book be both?"

I could but assure him that, in my time, I had faced

similar problems without ever finding their answers; and that, to the best of my judgment, even a book reviewer (who after all, howsoever staggering may seem the thought, is but mortal) may now and then be subject to mortal error.

However! my true point here is that I know of nothing more aidful to a creative writer than is a large deal of candid fault-finding with his book before it is published. For by this he may profit quite prodigally, if but upon the principle that two heads are better than one. And it was the best possible sort of relentless, microscopic fault-finding which, as had been the usage of Guy Holt, Stephen Benét now afforded me in his reports upon those three of my books which today make up the trilogy called Heirs and Assigns.

Through these reports I was brought without any paltering to see clearly what Benét objected to or had found inadequate, as well as just how in his opinion this passage or that entire episode might run improvingly; and while now and then I thought him in the wrong, and so let my text stand unaltered, yet for the most part I granted gladly the correctness of his carping; and with a lively gratitude I obliterated, or changed, or patched up, the offending feature before the story was printed.

Prior to all this, we had met briefly once or twice. I did not really know Stephen Benét as a person, however, until the January of 1941, when the Benét family convoked in the first American home of their ancestors, at St. Augustine in Florida; and there, for a week or so, he and I were much together. It was then that I asked him who was going to commemorate the adjacent St. Johns River in the Rivers of America series, of which at this time he and Carl Carmer were acting as the editors. And Benét's reply, here to phrase the affair with mildness, proved flabbergasting; for he said quietly,—

"Why don't you do it?"

Well, but because just for one reason, I told him (with some little doubt as to his sanity), it so happened that I did not know anything about the history of the St. Johns, or of Florida either, except for the Menéndez period only, between 1565 and 1574, this being an era which I had needed to study when I was writing *The First Gentleman of America.*

"Yes, but your friend Professor Hanna, to whom you dedicated the *First Gentleman,* knows all about Florida's history," Benét answered. "It is Hanna's specialty. And I was thinking that you and he might collaborate on the St. Johns."

Whereafter, and still speaking in that subdued and gentle manner which seemed to characterize him always, Benét went on with a quiet certitude to explain just what a magnificent chronicle I and Professor A. J. Hanna of Rollins College would be able to concoct between us; and I listened entranced, because the tall stoop-shouldered, owlish-eyed, quiet-voiced speaker was now making his hitherto incredible-seeming notion sound wholly plausible. I, in fact, question if in any of Stephen Benét's printed books you can find the imagination of a sterling poet moving with more charm or more forcefully, or more creatively, than it did upon that sunlit afternoon when the two of us were walking down St. George Street, and he depicted for my benefit that potential masterwork.

So I thought over his eloquence for a while; I then agreed to consult with Hanna as to the affair; and, in this way, did I by-and-by stand committed to share in completing the history of a river about which I knew virtually nothing.

And what in chief prompted me to the enterprise was my perception that history was about the only form of writing at which I had never tried my hand. Upon somewhat the same orderly principle that I have attempted to use for my so numerous books and trilogies titles beginning with every letter in the alphabet, so in the January of 1941 did I think it might be diverting to round off the catalogue of my writings by including among them a volume of history.

Well, and with the libraries of the Florida Historical Society and of the St. Augustine Historical Society and of Rollins College each at my disposal, I, within the next two years, had found out an astounding gallimaufry of data as to what had been going on upon or near the banks of the St. Johns ever since it was first discovered by Jean Ribaut upon the far-off May Day of

1562. And as befitted a Virginian, I was properly annoyed to observe that, within the confines of our nominal republic, a colony of Europeans, at St. Augustine in 1565, should have presumed to antedate Jamestown by some forty-odd years; as well as that, which seemed yet more headstrong, this colony had made bold to exist ever since then, so long after our, in comparison, parvenu Jamestown had been abandoned. As I have admitted in another place, it appears to any Virginian that such malapert doings fail to treat our official history of Virginia with a sufficient deference or suitably to honor our prized "priorities."

However, after having recovered to a modified extent from this impudent conduct upon the peninsula of Florida's part, I enjoyed my collaboration with my valued friend and fraternity brother, Professor Alfred Jackson Hanna, almost unreservedly. Almost, I say, because of the so many checks in its progress.

Thus, after we had once worked out the general outline of the book, then we needed to alter it from beginning to end, because of Hanna's politic afterthought that nothing of an unflattering tinge could be recorded as to any person whose descendants were as yet living in Florida and capable of becoming donors to Rollins College, the faculty of which he adorned; and after having agreed upon this tactful omission, we next began to differ constantly as to inclusions.

For but one example, it was my colleague's insistence that, since perhaps several of the lakes at Winter Park, surrounding Rollins College, at least possibly emptied through underground passages into the St. Johns River, our book in consequence ought to include an adequate history of Rollins College, say, about fifty or perhaps a hundred pages of it. He felt, and with emphasis, that in this manner to publicize his alma mater and his current employer could do no harm.

Well, and I honored his motives in the same instant that I firmly flouted their offspring, in the form of this notion; because since Rollins stood, as a crow flies in a cliché, some twenty-five miles from the St. Johns, and was in no whit or even in one half whit connected with it by any ancient or recent or present happenings, I could not see that to devote a large part of our book to Rollins and its academic glories could be justified by logic, or that for us to do so could fail to make for somewhat dull reading-matter.

Because what most impressed me in the past of the St. Johns was the startling number of more or less, but how far more more, grotesque persons who at various periods, and who in fact continually, had animated the evergreen banks and the sluggish surface of this memory-haunted river. To companion these fantastics with dullness I thought a crime. So I made plain to my collaborator this circumstance, some half dozen times, of necessity.

And Hanna agreed with me—by-and-by—that our book might advantageously become far less a formal history than a sort of chronological pageant of these so surprising persons, ranging from Jean Ribaut to Stephen Crane's widow, with history serving but as the backdrop against which their oddities would be made to stand out as boldly as we could manage. It was with this scheme in mind that we began and completed a volume which, whatsoever its demerits, may at least be termed unique in the Rivers of America series. And once fairly started upon this book, we both got an exceeding zest out of its writing, yes, even out of our continuous but wholly affable squabbles with each other over what to include and what to omit—with Stephen Benét officiating from afar as our referee.

For he had now returned to New York City; and the successive sections of *The St. Johns,* as Hanna and I wrote severally, and then the other rewrote, its various chapters in Florida or in Virginia (so far out of their proper order that the first and second chapters were the last to be done), were sent on in batches for Benét to criticize. And his acute, patient, endless notes, in reply to each batch, found fault most freely with everything from our sentiments to our syntax, as well as criticasting our plausibility and the expedience of a few passages, with a painstaking which delighted, at any rate, me. (Hereabouts I cannot answer for Hanna, inasmuch as a pedagogue, howsoever unassuming by nature, may well become so used to giving over each workday to setting straight the errors of other persons that to find the process reversed may appear to him anarchic.) And almost all of Benét's emendments we adopted, so that before long he was in reality a co-author of *The St. Johns.*

The typescript of the final text of this so frequently pulled about and argued over and re-revised book went forward to Farrar & Rinehart's by express on or about the tenth of March 1943; and upon the thirteenth of that month our radio, in the afternoon while I was shaving and listening to a news program in St. Augustine, reported the death of Stephen Vincent Benét from heart failure during the day's early morning hours just after his going to bed for the night.

I was stunned. I, in truth, was profoundly horrified by the unexpectedness of this announcement as to one whom, for all that I had seen or talked with him so little, I felt to be a personal friend and my benefactor. And yet another uncanny surprise awaited me when, two days later, the afternoon mail brought in a letter from the Steve Benét whom I knew to have been buried that same morning.

It had been written and addressed and sealed and duly stamped by him but an hour or thereabouts before his fatal heart attack, so I discovered later; and being found upon his desk, it was mailed to me a brief while after his death. And its debonair foreplanning of the future I could not but in the circumstances esteem tragic.

This letter, which I am re-reading today, professed its writer's pleasure to hear that "all is well and the St. Johns flowing North"; for my announcement that the final complete typescript of the book had been dispatched had reached Benét upon the last day of his life.

And the only letter which I have ever received from a dead man continued:—

"The manuscript should be in my hands in a few days and I'll be very glad to see it. I recognize the difficulties of collaboration, but you have every reason to be proud of the result. It is a fine book—and it is a contribution to history. And people are going to steal from it."

Well, and howsoever over-charitably Benét may have erred in descriptiveness, yet was he correct in this oddly irrelevant sounding prophecy, I needs mention here; for at least two highly popular and vilely written historical romances have been borrowed from, or rather they have been based on, parts of *The St. Johns* since it was published.

His letter then thanked me for the patience with which, during the book's completion, I had endured his "various editorial cries and yells"—which, heaven knows, I had always found to be no less diverting than helpful—thence going on to promise that, in spite of war-time restrictions, he would see, somehow, to the book's having a handsome enough appearance.

And so forth and so on. It, in brief, was just a pleasant friendly letter, casual and light-hearted. But it did not at all elate me. I, instead, was finding my circumstances somewhat grisly, thus to have a dead man jesting with me, as it were, from the grave into which he had been lowered but an hour or two earlier. Moreover, I both liked and admired Stephen Benét; and upon him—whom I hardly knew as a person, but only through his letters—I had come to rely as a disembodied and invaluable, unsparing sage counsellor.

And to his memory I remain grateful. He aided me beyond any athletics of rhetoric in polishing off the trilogy known as Heirs and Assigns. Whereas, but for him, no line of the trilogy called It Happened in Florida would ever have existed. His notion it was entirely which set me to writing about the St. Johns River, and which thus prompted my attendant two years' study of Floridian history; and in this studying I encountered, and I was allured by, the legends of Gasparilla and of the Arredondos. These stories had, it is true, no link with the St. Johns, and I ran across them but by chance; my aforementioned Scots thrift, however, pronounced them by far too engaging to be wasted. And thus, by-and-by, I was using them for the cornerstones of *There Were Two Pirates* and of *The Devil's Own Dear Son*.

Yes; I owe a profound deal to Stephen Vincent Benét, in that he changed and recolored, and always improvingly, one of my trilogies throughout; and was the immediate if haphazard cause of still another trilogy. Not many writers are responsible to this extent for six entire books by a fellow practitioner. So it follows that, out of plain honesty, I have a need in these pages to include him among my so very various unacknowledged collaborators—along with Guy Holt, and with John Farrar, and with both of my wives, and with, as I rather think, my grandmother likewise—and that I cherish with a lively fondness all my but too scanty memories of Stephen Vincent Benét.

30

Speaks with Candor of a Great Lady

To HARK back, then, I have not, with an actual intimacy, known in the flesh many writers who were at all widely acknowledged as auctorial. But my one remaining as yet undiscussed collaborator in polite letters—who was Ellen Glasgow—I did know, it is my belief, more thoroughly and more comprehendingly, if but because in more varied phases, than did any other human being during the last twenty years of her living.

And in her I did not ever encounter, of course, quite the personage whom she depicted in Ellen Glasgow's autobiography, that beautiful and wise volume which contains a large deal of her very best fiction. Nor did this fact surprise me when I came to read *The Woman Within*. I have spoken earlier of the imaginative fashion in which every writer of true distinction will invariably handle his, or her, own personal past.

For this reason, I intend hereinafter to disregard *The Woman Within*. I say merely that it is a book

217

wherein many matters in which I had a share, or about which I happened to know personally, have been— whether in the behalf of kindliness or of art or of pathos—so very freely recolored that I distrust the entire book throughout as a factual record. I elect to applaud it rather as a work of genius and as a volume well worthy of its writer.

Which is saying a great deal; yet as to my admiration of Ellen Glasgow's literary talents and of these talents' exercise I have borne witness in another place; and to everything which I have written concerning her in *Let Me Lie* I adhere.

By and large, I believe her to have excelled all the other feminine novelists whom America has produced; and, with this verdict, Ellen Glasgow found no quarrel herself, except that she liked better to omit from it the word "feminine." But then she did not think over highly, no, not ever in private conversation, of any novelist anywhere who risked being alive and more or less prominent at the time she was speaking; death alone could invoke an amnesty, or if the atonement were sufficiently by-past, even out-and-out laudations. For a dead novelist was no longer her rival.

Me, however, she could condone upon the ground of my not writing novels but merely romances which did not attempt to handle actual life; our books were in no way competitors; and after having thought up this distinction, I stayed at some pains to emphasize it in all my dealings with her. So we got on excellently, even though I well knew, from the benign tale-bearing of our joint friends, that, when I was absent, her remarks concerning me, now and then at least, were affably derogative. For I delighted always in Ellen Glasgow, even in her display of qualities which a precisian might not find admirable; and her shrewishness in discussing any living writer of some supposed eminence was alike the arena of a keen wit and a never-failing well-spring of diverting malice.

And besides that, in her I felt a sort of genial proprie-tary interest, because in, at any rate, one bit of literary advisement I had been to her enduringly helpful. There can be no damage, now that Ellen Glasgow's repute as a "social historian" has been made unassailable and a conceded matter of course in so very many summaries of American literature, and by so numerous theses and doctoral dissertations, in the confession that I aided in evoking for her this nowadays time-honored epithet, which I take to be deathless so long as her name sur-vives.

For during the early summer of 1928 I reminded Ellen that, when reviewing *Barren Ground* for the *Na-tion,* during the May of 1925, I had expressed my large, personal admiration of the completeness with which her books, as a whole, presented "a portrayal of social and economic Virginia since the War Between the States."

Well, and so did I urge her, this notion of your

books' containing an all-around social and economic portrayal of our native state is quite highly imposing. It
is a notion which really ought not to be wasted. So
now that Doubleday is to bring out a definitive edition
of your books, why do you not use this notion? Why,
very much as I have arranged my own books as a Biography of the Life of Manuel, do you not henceforward
describe your various novels as "a social history of Virginia"? The first two of them, by ill luck, cannot be included under this heading; but upon the others it
would bestow an invaluable effect of edifying profound-
ness and of unity.

And Ellen upon reflection saw my point. She agreed
dubiously as to its possibilities. Then she enkindled
to them cannily. And it followed that in 1929, in a
preface added to *The Battle-Ground,* she adopted my
notion in what I thought to be a small bland masterpiece.

For this preface explained that *The Battle-Ground,*
as published in 1902, was the earliest in a series of
novels which, several years prior to 1902, its future
writer had then hoped would become, in time, "a complete social history of Virginia since the Civil War";
and that, in this now pretty well advanced "comedy of
manners which would embrace the whole varied struc-
ture of Virginian society," each of the author's other
novels as issued between 1902 and 1929 had formed
a chapter. And everywhere the intelligentsia accepted
quite gravely this somewhat belated exposition of the
nature of Ellen Glasgow's books and of their underly-

ing unity, just as she and I had hoped would be the outcome.

It followed also that, a while later on, it became my privilege to assist in the selecting and the grouping of Ellen Glasgow's better novels so as to make them conform as nearly as might be with this resonant notion of a social history when this notion flowered so handsomely through an edition of luxury which included and classified twelve of her books as "a Social History of Virginia from the decade before the Confederacy."

I had likewise a joyous hand in revising somewhat thoroughly each of the prefaces which were then written, or extended, for the selected novels, and in which, with an increasing explicitness, was stressed this impressive and so well sounding notion until Ellen Glasgow herself became convinced, in all honestness, I know, that ever since 1899 she had been at work on "a social history in the more freely interpretative form of fiction." And equally was everybody else convinced also.

I still like to remember that.

And I like, too, to remember that I was of some little service to Ellen Glasgow in the autumn of 1940 when, after her second heart attack, her health had collapsed, leaving her unable to deal any further with the rough draft of *In This Our Life*. The book meant a vast and a poignant deal to Ellen, because of the fact's being accepted everywhere, by all those who bother about such matters, that her next novel was scheduled to receive a Pulitzer prize. Indeed this fact had been conveyed to her, in some way and I do not know how, semi-officially. Here, then, was awaiting a distinction for which she hungered angrily, with a righteous and a more than justified resentment of the twenty years throughout which it had been withheld. And now, upon the brink of triumph, she was not bodily able to finish, or rather, to put into any acceptable shape, a final draft of the book which would ensure this distinction.

So I remedied affairs by doing this revising for her, in chief out of love and friendship and my honest sympathy, but in some part out of the derisive pleasure which I got from knowing that at long last I was completing a Pulitzer prize winner.

For these reasons then did I more than gladly give over some three or four months to *In This Our Life,* or to be more accurate, the afternoons of these months, because, in the mornings of them, I was drafting *The First Gentleman of America.* And I found it droll enough to be at work simultaneously upon two fictions so diverse.

My collaborator in writing the more important of them all this while stayed an invalid; but twice a week I would visit Ellen Glasgow's sick chamber at about four o'clock in the afternoon, so as to show her what changes and slight amendments I was making in her text; and she, propped up in bed, wan and emaciated but as vigorous of mind as ever, would applaud them for the most part. She balked now and then, however, and as I thought ill-advisedly, over what she took to be a touch of the too frivolous or of the slightly risqué; for to my finding, this novel required a deal of animating; but meekly I would shrug and accept her mandates as to what, after all, was going to be her book, and not mine.

Then, still at Ellen's bedside, I would have my old-fashioned cocktail toward half-past five o'clock, an indulgence which, throughout that autumn, her doctors denied her; and we would speak viciously concerning one or more of our joint literary acquaintances, as in those unregenerate times was the manner of any two authors when they conferred genially in private. Here was a sport at which she by far excelled me, as I observed with envy; but we enjoyed to the full those verbal battues none the less. And after that, I would kiss her cheek and depart with a fresh batch of typescript for me to revise and to make tidy during the next three or four days.

I like nowadays to recall that I was privileged to complete this trivial yet not unlaborious taskwork for Ellen Glasgow's comfort and her ultimate glory. It would be pleasing too, to my self-conceit, to believe that *In This Our Life* was thus made her very best novel; but, unluckily, the book is amenable to no such describing by anybody. After all, though, it did win for her the long-coveted Pulitzer prize in 1942—that being the first year in which, as Ellen remarked with venom, this guerdon had been reduced from a thousand dollars to

an invidious five hundred, and—which was far worse—
a full twenty years after it had been awarded to Willa
Cather.

Nobody anywhere who, at any time, heard Ellen
Glasgow discourse and dilate as to the exact literary
merits of Willa Cather, is likely not to have recalled
forever the speaker's eloquence. Here is a matter which
a great while afterward I discussed with Henry Seidel
Canby, I remember; and we both spoke with awed admiration.

In fact, I like nowadays to bear in mind every item
of my long association with Ellen Glasgow and of our
two decades of intimacy, an intimacy which was as
complete, I believe, as could very well exist between her
and any other person.

For one matter, I was made privy even to the surprising fact that, unlike a majority of all the other authors
whom I have met, she, in reality, stayed somewhat, or
at least relatively, humble-minded as to her books' actual merit. The most of them were honest and often
excellent work. She knew that, and she admired a fair
number of her publishings with a lenient candor. But
she knew also, at bottom, that not even her best books
were quite as good as she was determined everybody
should believe them to be.

Yes, and in this determination she was resolute with
a completeness I found pathetic. For her books were in
a singular degree the summing up of all that Ellen
Glasgow's life amounted to—in chief, because her pre-

mature, well-nigh total deafness had isolated her from life's normal activities, or from any untrammeled intercourse with human beings. That was her tragedy always, or at any rate, from but shortly after her attainment of womanhood. She was already hard of hearing at barely twenty-four, I remember, when I, who at the time was an undergraduate of William and Mary, first talked with her in the May of 1898, in Williamsburg, among circumstances such as she has depicted with a reasonable accurateness; and this ailment increased, relentlessly.

None who ever met Ellen Glasgow can well have forgotten the hearing aid upon which by-and-by she was dependent until very near the end of her existence on earth. Only within the last two years of her life, when her health had failed completely and she had become well-nigh house-bound, did she secure a machine which was both efficient and virtually imperceptible; whereas the hearing aid that she employed in the era of her prime had stayed deplorably far from being either.

It resembled a portable small telephone which she carried in her hand, and which a cord attached to her person somehow; and into the receiver of which you had to talk directly, at rather close quarters. She could not hear anything whatever except the voice of someone who was speaking thus. It required a long time for anybody to become so far accustomed to this device as to be able to speak at all naturally to her while she held the receiver pointed toward you. And in company there, of course, was no foretelling toward whom she would next point this receiver. That was rather upsetting.

"It rattled me completely," so I was told by one of her former guests, long after Ellen Glasgow's death, "when at the dinner table she would make some brilliant remark and then aim that telephone thing at me all of a sudden and wait smilingly for me to telephone back. I felt it was my turn now to say something very witty, and I simply couldn't ever think of anything."

Well, and all strangers, or relative strangers, must have felt more or less the same way, one imagines. Even her intimates found that to talk with her in private, for any considerable while, was a strain. In this way did her deafness remain always as a continuous barrier to any frank contacts with her fellow creatures. Here was a fact which she knew over clearly. And it followed that she would permit no reference to be made by anybody whatever, except only herself now and then, to her deafness, as well as that she regarded her deafness as a plain proof of heaven's malignity.

Meanwhile, she had, as concerned her daily life in Richmond, no women acquaintances with whom she could, or with whom she did, pretend to meet as her equals either in spirit or in mind. All the contemporaneous and younger members of her somewhat huge family she had found uncongenial, with but two exceptions. Every one of the others, whether alive or entombed, she disliked without any special concealment.

She revered the memory of her long dead mother, but that of her father she detested. I did not know why, during her lifetime, because more than once I declined to let her tell me, remarking prudishly that, to my mind, all such ungracious topics were better left untouched by the tongue of filial propriety.

Then there was yet another matter which, through my stolid election rather than by Ellen's own choice, we never talked about. I mean that somewhat often she implied her girlhood and her past in general to have been a constant entanglement, or say, a true tropical torrid jungle, of love-affairs which, at the moment, she was not unwilling to discuss; and I then sheered off invariably. Do you preserve these fictions, I exhorted, to lend zest to your autobiography! I did not ever encourage Ellen Glasgow to embellish—as toward our late middle life we need all come to do, through proper pride—the memories of one's youth's amorous adventurings and of youth's love-dealings which, while enjoyable enough at the time, yet in reality fail always to equal that which we had expected in the way of rapture. I knew that Ellen—and howsoever unconfined or how vestal-like her amours—would not have spoken the truth hereabouts any more than does anyone else.

In brief, then, during the while that I observed this lonely and baffled woman, her writing and the applause of her writing were the sole matters which concerned Ellen Glasgow vitally.

Well, and in consequence she became for her writ-

ing the most consummate impresario that our age has
known. Nor am I forgetting George Bernard Shaw,
whose buffooneries, while aidful enough in all democ-
racies, of which the inhabitants foster and obey that
mental average which has furthered our world's present-
day resemblance to Utopia, were crude and raucous
when likened to the methods of Ellen Glasgow.

For always, to anyone who could abet the popular
success of her books, she was affability's self, without
any least hint of truckling or of cajolement, but rather
with the benignness of a *grande dame* who condescends
thus graciously because of her unique liking for you
personally. And you felt honored by it perforce. You
basked in its radiancy. There was no possible resisting
the charm of her superb courteousness and comradeship
and of her special confidence in you.

So, then, at one time or another she had as her
house guest, or she at least entertained palatially as her
guest of honor at a dinner party, almost every practicing
literary critic in the United States who possessed any
considerable influence. She was no less handsomely
hospitable to a large number of authors of fair distinction—provided only that the latter were disposed now
and then to write book reviews or an article on current
reading-matter. And she so charmed them all that, after
leaving her presence, they very nearly every one of
them at once published with enthusiasm a pæan or two
in praise of her novels. It reminded you of Circe, the
way in which Ellen Glasgow transformed her guests,
not into beasts but into press agents. As I remember

matters, among the literati thus feted, Joseph Hergesheimer alone, for some reason or another, did not succumb to her magic-working. The others wrote lauda-
tory articles about Ellen Glasgow.

And at bottom she regarded almost every one of
these her pleased playthings with a more or less amiable
contempt. I am reminded hereabouts of many and
more instances of her magnetism's success, some of
which I would cite but for the fear of seeming spiteful
as to a performance which from the bottom of my heart
I admired and applauded. When Ellen Glasgow thus
hunted after an advantageous publicity, she was doing
that which in some degree has been attempted by every
living writer whom I have observed (and do you believe me that I have properly observed myself), with
the sole difference that Ellen Glasgow did it far more
adroitly, in the very best vein of polite comedy. And if
her acting was perfect, so, too, was its stage setting.

For the visiting literary critic would enter an ample
early Victorian home which had every air of being
ancestral. He would find it equipped throughout with
antique furnishings, all in flawless condition, which
might very well have been long-treasured Glasgovian
heirlooms. He would properly admire their superabun-
dance, the fruitage of none knew how many centuries
of aristocratic opulence. And he would be suitably impressed, even awed a bit, perhaps, by this staidly luxuri-
ous and picturesque survival of the Old South.

So he would babble about it in print afterward, telling you how—I cite an instance—"in the great square,

high-ceilinged rooms, hung with ancestral portraits and quaint engravings and furnished with old pieces of Sheraton, Chippendale and Heppelwhite, Ellen Glasgow entertains her friends in the grand manner."

And if a skilled actress graced this not uncarefully devised stage setting, so did a very great woman. I have touched here upon her jealousy of any potential rival in polite letters and upon her genial, all-pardonable, slight tireless hypocrisy in furthering her books' success, alike as masterpieces and as merchandise, because I know that, in the last outcome, both of these qualities worked for good. The jealousy spurred her into trying to write better than did these possible rivals, and for the most part to succeed in this attempt; whereas, the high drawing-room comedy of her acting was philanthropic in that it gave pleasure to all her auditors and promoted the fame of many novels which well deserved a wide recognition. I am not saying that jealousy and a politic dissimulation should be called out-and-out virtues; but merely that inasmuch as, in this special instance, all their effects were beneficial, by nobody should they be termed vices, or even faults. And so, for one, I commend without stint the exercise of these qualities in this special and all-remunerative instance.

These qualities were, in any case, an essential part of Ellen Glasgow, a part which, if left unweighed, leaves a great woman uncomprehended. A great woman, I repeat! Whether or not she will prove an enduring writer stays, as with all other modern authors, just anybody's guess. But as to Ellen Glasgow's having been

a distinctive, nay, a gorgeous personality, there can be
no dispute.

She was of handsome person, a person which she
dressed to full advantage. She appeared, to my continual wonderment, to have read everything ever published. Her tact was unfailing. She had wit and charm
and learning and (apart from her pathological hatred
of a literary rival) a generousness which was illimitable.
As concerned dumb animals—but above all, dogs—her
sympathy reached, and even a bit overlapped, the sentimental; so that to ensure their well-being she gave
prodigally both of time and money. She was no less
free-handed nor less energetic as to helping the ill or
the indigent among her fellow creatures. To a beginning author so long as he stayed uncelebrated she was
profuse alike in encouragement and in sound advice
and in blandly exaggerative encomia to be used in ad-
vertising his book. She was frankly and frigidly exclu-
sive as to which inhabitants of Richmond she would
allow to enter her impressive mansion as social equals;
but, otherwise, she revelled in kindliness to everybody.
And so, for one, I both loved and I admired this affably
unconscientious woman always.

I admired her, too, not merely as a person and as a
writer, but because, unlike Guy Holt and John Macy,
she had made of her literary gifts the very utmost conceivable. For it is my fixed faith, I can but repeat, that
the possessor of such gifts lives under an unterrene
obligation to develop them to the full. And should the
doing of this entail a little chicanery, why, then I con-

fess to no more abhorrence than I can cherish against
Edmund Waller for his time-serving or François de
Montcorbier Villon for his pimping or Algernon
Charles Swinburne for his alcoholism. Each of these
men, even through these special vices, was still nour-
ishing and enlarging and exercising more vividly his
gifts as a writer. And by my faith that is what they
ought to have done.

Yet there is, of course, no justifying this faith, not
by any common-sense standards. That is why I have
granted that Holt and Macy may well have chosen the
more wisely when they neglected this faith, and thus
at least were spared the prolonged slaving which its
honoring evokes and makes continual. But I think that
Ellen Glasgow chose, and by long odds, the more ad-
mirably when she elected to serve this faith by any and
all possible polite methods.

She wanted always, I mean, to make of her gifts as a
writer the utmost. She labored always toward this goal.
And she attained it.

She wanted also—or rather, she tacitly and sullenly
demanded of heaven, I think—as an atoning for the
normal pleasures and the normal ties and the normal
contacts with her fellow beings which circumstances
had denied her, fame and daily applause. And these,
too, she attained. She enjoyed her famousness; she very
much liked her medals, her awards, her prizes, her
honorary college degrees, and her yet other tinsel trib-
utes; but she remained always, during at any rate the

last twenty years of her life, an unhappy woman, resentful of that which she—still sullenly, but far from tacitly—esteemed to be the outrageous unfairness of heaven in heaven's traffic with Ellen Glasgow.

Being a famous writer, in short, did not bring to her any more abiding happiness than it brought to Sinclair Lewis. And so, in considering these two among my former acquaintances, I dare to doubt if ever, just in itself, the consciousness of being a literary success, howsoever ardently that attained goal may have been desired and nobly labored for with a scorn of all other goals, has at any time contented anybody.

An Afterword Ending with Gratitude

Yes, and my doubt as to any such possible contentment at once hales back my thinking to that volume called *Quiet, Please* which led me into recording these random reflections as to affairs and persons I once liked and still like to remember, in chief because of the part they had in my writing; and in which book I prattled unblushingly about my own aforetime quite general famousness as a writer, and stated several reasons for my being well enough satisfied, upon the whole, to have outlived it.

Yet I need here to add that the main trouble with my special sort of literary eminence—not among the intelligent, I am so vainglorious as to hope, but among far too many other and more widely influential classes —was that I felt I had not earned my celebrity with fairness or through any personal achievement. It more or less troubled my conscience to reflect that after eighteen years of unsuccess I had become temporarily famous through accident, or rather, now that I reconsider this ancient farce, through the distressing tend-

234

ency of persons quite other than myself to obey the call of duty.

For the press agent of a cheap-jack vaudeville house, at the beck of his salaried duty to advertise his theatre, composed during the Christmas holidays of 1919 an imaginative account of how a recently published romance, because of its extreme sensuality and moral corruption, and "its deft and knowing treatment of all the perversities, abnormalities and damn-foolishness of sex," was being read with zest by even the more illiterate underlings of Broadway's theatrical world. They were all exhorting one another, so did his fancy report:—

"Say, kid, get a book called *Jurgen!* It gets away with murder!"

And this extravaganza was printed forthwith, upon 3 January 1920, by a newspaper columnist in order to make more sprightly, and to flavor with the scandalous, his column. Each man, you see, was but performing the duties of his office and earning his family's bread and butter.

Well, and this fantasy, inasmuch as it appeared in a reputable and a widely circulated newspaper, was noted by various pillars of the New York Society for the Suppression of Vice. And they—most naturally without ever contaminating their staid minds by reading *Jurgen*—at once fulfilled their social duty, as high-salaried and therefore responsible citizens, by calling upon their representative hired agent to suppress any such nefarious filth as was threatening to corrupt Broadway's morals. He thereupon (as I need not tell you, was his obvious duty) obeyed his employers' orders by seizing my publishers' as yet unsold copies of *Jurgen* and procuring an indictment against my publishers for vending an obscene, lewd, lascivious and indecent book.

Everyone involved, in brief, was but hearkening, most praiseworthily, and with a proper deference, to the voice of his paid-for personal duty.

The publicity resultant from all these virtuous doings helped me among no few of those intelligent and literate persons who thus first heard about my existence; and who, after reading *Jurgen* (of which some 4000 copies were still in circulation) failed to be either shocked or titillated sensually. A gratifying number of them considered the aspersed romance to display some literary merit; they championed it nobly; and they made inquiries as to my other publishings.

My eleven preceding books in this way, for the first time since I had begun writing books a bit over eighteen years earlier, reached more than a scant dozen or so attentive readers. By some of these readers I was ranked as a writer of importance; and my books began to sell in increasing quantities. Temporarily, I was respected loudly by the intelligentsia; schoolchildren wrote asking for my autograph; and, as an author, I became a commercial success. All which was pleasant enough.

To the other side, among my new-found patrons there were many, and very many, lecherous-minded persons who had read *Jurgen* solely in quest of its reputed obscenity; and who, discovering passages in which they maintained the existence of two meanings, preferred the more indelicate one. They found also that, through the virtually simple process of substituting for various nouns included in the text of *Jurgen* some quite other noun such as was more familiar to the walls of a public privy than to drawing-rooms, a number of passages could be made phallic. They found all this to be appliable to yet other romances by me—without bothering to reflect that, as I pointed out in *Taboo*, this is an exegesis equally remunerative when applied to the rhymes of Mother Goose—or for that matter, to most of the hundred and fifty Psalms of David, King over Israel, or to the four books of Euclid.

So among this class of, so to speak indulgently, human beings, I was but too soon a bit over-well advertised as a consistently indecent writer; by the more freely imaginative of them the mild and provincial gossip of Richmond, as to the misdemeanors and vices and crimes of my private life, was seized upon and so very gorgeously re-embroidered as to become Neronean and nation-wide; and among coprophilic morons all these malodors clung to me and to my writings for a considerable number of years, long after a trial in open court had exonerated *Jurgen* of perniciousness. The reading public of America, in its inferior strata, does not readily succumb to a change of what have been termed, and quite gravely too, the ideas of these lower strata.

Now it so happened that, through what I still believe

to have been no unusual quirk of human nature, I did not enjoy being made notorious among the semi-illiterate as a purveyor of sly indecencies and a practitioner of all known iniquities. I disliked, and it may have been even a trifle peevishly, the intrusive hordes of idiots and prurient fools, of busybodies, of unpublished authors well worthy of that condition, of dabblers in black magic, of catamites and of amateur strumpets—all which delinquents and rabble and bobtail, Coolidge then being consul, henceforward for a full, fretful fifteen years or more, molested me and interfered with my opportunities to write in quiet. The attentiveness, nay, the homage, of such human refuse bothered me.

Today they, almost every one of them, or to be more accurate, their children and their grandchildren, let me alone; their babbling, wide-eyed unannounced visits, or their afflictive visitations rather, have ceased; and the postman no longer toils toward my front door bearing his daily armful of inane lewd rhapsodies, whether of acclaim or of pious denouncing, and of invitations to this or to the other carnal sportiveness—such letters, in brief, as I have indicated in *These Restless Heads* and again in *Special Delivery*. And for these varied forms of relief I am grateful.

Some persons here and there are still pleased to like at least some of my books; and concerning them they now and then write to me, as I think, intelligently. I, at any rate, enjoy their not over-cloyingly frequent letters; and this was not true of a majority of the thousands—or was it millions?—of letters which I received during my heyday as an allegedly daring and immoral and lascivious author. I, to the contrary, found it humiliating, and in a mild degree enraging, to be pestered, but, above all, to be admired, by such riffraff as must have written most of these letters. And today I am grateful that now not for a fair while have I been bothered by many of these obscene outpourings. Sparsely they arrive even nowadays, such is the force of tradition, but not in a sufficient quantity to be annoying.

Another facet of the trouble was that I, who by nature was born bashful and as continent as befitted a Virginian, and no less befittingly respectful of all social conventions, could not but feel myself, in the role of a daring and immoral and lascivious desperado, to be miscast. It was a part I could never hope to adorn. And, inasmuch as before the beginning of my notoriousness I had already entered into my forties, and was both contentedly and overmasteringly married, I could not look forward to becoming by-and-by, not even through the most heroic efforts, anything like such a devil of a fellow in fact as I was in scandal, I would reflect almost wistfully.

Yes; I am afraid that at times I was just a tiny bit envious of the Cabell of popular myth, that all-defiant rake-hellion. He so far outdwarfed the graying burgess I found in the mirror. And thus today I am glad to be rid of his overshadowing. The flamboyant knave bothered me.

Well, but today, now that I am no longer world-famous, all these annoyances have departed. I do not any longer need to worry over the exact mental or moral status of persons who like my books, nor over my failure, as an individual, to outrival Don Juan or Lucifer, nor in fact to worry about anything in particular, inasmuch as my main desire of life has been granted me—to complete the work which I had hoped to accomplish, in the Biography of the Life of Manuel and in the various other groups of my writings, more or less just as I first planned it all.

When I reflect upon the half-century of pleasure which I have derived from mustering into print these cohorts, then the question does not in the least seem to matter, whether some few or none of these books will endure. I, here to become colloquial, I have had my fun, either way. That suffices me. And my conscience tells me, complacently enough, that I have made the most of my talents, such as they happened to be. For their limitations I disclaim being responsible.

What alone troubles me is that, after fifty-odd years of writing books, it seems odd not still to be about that loved labor. For to write (and then to rewrite), I can but repeat, has been to me a demented and bedrugged enjoyment, relished almost sensuously, and yet with an underlying sense of fulfilling my supreme duty, of doing what I was meant for. I would like to go on with it. So at times do I envy Walter Savage Landor, who wrote until eighty-nine; and George Bernard Shaw, who went on until ninety-four; but above all, Moses-ben-Amram, who did not relinquish active authorship until his years were an hundred and twenty.

But I may not hope for any such prolonged self-indulgence, the more thanks to the progress of modern science. Which means that, after having been properly dosed, under the most advanced medical auspices, with two of the very latest wonder drugs, I was so ill-advised some little while ago as to prove allergic to both of them.

That this was awkward, my physicians admitted quite civilly. They did not blame me, or at least not openly, for failing to respond in a correct manner to the proper treatment. With a noble broadmindedness they, instead, admitted that the main trouble with these antibiotics was that they so often killed the patient or else left him permanently, as in my case, a notably impermanent invalid. It was just one of those things, they assured me cheerily, which doctors have to put up with.

That, then, is how my health and the strength to write yet another trilogy or so were taken away from me. That is why I may not ever hope, during the next fifty years or thereabouts, to deride Moses. But the books which I needed to write—the Biography and the six trilogies—have all been completed. My body has well served my turn.

And by no means do I make haste to intone *Nunc dimittis* now that (still at a sad variance with Moses) my eye is undeniably dimmed and my natural force is abated. To the contrary: for in a sedate and a genteel and, or so do I flatter myself, an as yet but slightly doddering fashion, I continue to enjoy the fag-end of my quiet existence here upon earth. More lucky than was more majestic Ellen Glasgow or than world-applauded homeless Hal Lewis, I have today, as I have always had, a sufficiency of normal pleasures and of human ties and of intimate contacts. Or in fact, for a person of my restricted sociability, I now and then believe myself to be endowed with a small excess of these blessings. My wife is addicted to having in just a few friends without any warning whatever.

I in brief—here to sum up everything—I have lived a rather long while as mortality goes; and I have liked living. I have always liked it, by and large. I have liked human beings, as a slightly foreign genus, without finding any need to admire every one of them as flawless. But, above all, I have liked writing books.

And as I have tried to show you in this special volume, I have liked a great many of my assistants and of my collaborators and of my competitors in writing books. Nor have I, in any manner, hidden away from you the fact that I have liked also the two women who married me, and who both of them, in addition to their more serious-minded activities, have helped me to write books. I suppose that, in a way, I even liked, or at least was flattered by, the repute of being a noteworthy author, once upon a departed time, howsoever interminably the role turned out to be a nuisance.

At all events, I observe that, in life's evening, I cannot subscribe to the perhaps over-popular sentiment, "God, but isn't life awful!" I have found life opulent in affairs and people that I have liked and like to remember. And even though I may still harbor some little uncertainty as to His precise purpose or nature or future intentions, yet do I praise with fervor Whosoever may be responsible for the universe which I have been permitted for perhaps an irrational deal more than my deserved share of years to inhabit and so very often to find pleasurable and droll.

EXPLICIT